Praise for Lead Like It Matters... Because It Does

"Just when you think there is little new to say about leadership, Roxi Hewertson has created this groundbreaking work. I've never seen anything like it. The conceptual framework is powerful, practical, and personal. It introduces an innovative, step-by-step, developmental approach providing the reader not just insightful understanding about how to lead, but a sequence of exercises applying each new concept. It reflects a lifetime of learning by doing. For those who follow its counsel, *Lead Like It Matters* is transformative."

—Richard McDaniel, Chairman, Collegiate Retail Alliance, Inc., and coauthor of *Measure What Matters*

"Roxi gets it! If you want a compendium of current thought about leadership, this is it. With a keen grasp of where modern leadership is, Roxi has created a readable roadmap for those who want to take the trip."

—Rodney Napier, PhD, Principle, The Napier Group, and coauthor of *Groups: Theory and Experience*

"*Lead Like It Matters...Because It Does* is full of aha moments and jam packed with practical and deeply researched leadership insights that will positively and immediately transform your work environment."

—Louise Phipps Senft, Phipps Senft Institute for Relational Leadership

"Roxi has given us the valuable and practical must dos, nice to dos, and really don't dos of being an effective leader and creating an enthusiastic and high performance team based on sound theory and solid experience."

—Tom DeCotiis, PhD, Cofounder of Corvirtus, LLC and author of *Make It Glow: How to Build a Company Reputation for Human Goodness, Flawless Execution and Being Best-in-Class.*

"Roxi is so right! If only our country's leaders would all read *Lead Like It Matters...Because It Does* and learn from Roxi's insights and experience to lead with courage and compassion."

—Deborah C. Hoard, President, PhotoSynthesis Productions

"*Lead Like It Matters...Because It Does* is NOT a book that you will read through and put on your shelf. It is a playbook that you will consistently refer to on your leadership journey. You will come to understand your strengths and opportunities as a leader—and most importantly have a clear path to make improvements in your own performance. The chapters are designed so that you can easily find the skill sets and exercises you want to revisit. Roxi has created dozens of engaging exercises and real-life stories to help you navigate the messy world of leading people and teams."

—Deborah Howard, CEO and Andréa Catizone,
President of Senior Living SMART

"This book is FULL of leadership insights and practicality. You will enjoy and profit from Roxi's wisdom and humanity."

—Robert J. Fersh, President and Founder
of Convergence Center for Policy Resolution

"I immediately began using the tools Roxi suggested to improve my communication, collaboration, and relationships; it's paid off over and over!"

—Amy Berg, Associate Provost SUNY Cortland

"*Lead Like It Matters...Because It Does* offers new and seasoned leaders a very practical road map to effective leadership in today's fast-paced and complex world."

—Carola Weil, PhD, Dean, School of Professional
and Extended Studies American University

"Finally a book that delivers on its promise! Roxi provides advice that any leader on any level can benefit from, and more importantly, implement."

—Raoul Davis, CEO Ascendant Group

"Drawing on her vast experience, Roxi's book provides a clear and compelling guide for personal leadership development—and a continuous journey of discovery and insight."

—Carl Haynes PhD, President, Tompkins-Cortland
Community College

"Roxi's book provided me with the knowledge and realistic steps that have guided me to real and positive change in my life and career."

—Bridget Rigas, VP for Communications and Development,
Boyce Thompson Institute

"An essential tool for achieving individual leadership effectiveness, *Lead Like It Matters...Because It Does* guides readers on an in-depth exploration of the values and experiences defining them as leaders; revealing how to best leverage one's unique approach to maximize individual and organizational performance."

—Nathan Ives, President and CEO, StrategyDriven Enterprises

Lead Like It Matters...

Because It Does

Lead Like It Matters...
Because It Does

Practical Leadership Tools
to Inspire and Engage Your People
and Create Great Results!

ROXI BAHAR HEWERTSON

New York   Chicago   San Francisco   Athens   London
Madrid   Mexico City   Milan   New Delhi
Singapore   Sydney   Toronto

1 2 3 4 5 6 7 8 9 0   DOC/DOC   1 2 0 9 8 7 6 5 4

ISBN 978-0-07-183302-8
MHID 0-07-183302-1

e-ISBN 978-0-07-183303-5
e-MHID 0-07-183303-X

Library of Congress Cataloging-in-Publication Data
Bahar Hewertson, Roxi.
   Lead like it matters—because it does : practical leadership tools to inspire and engage your people and create great results / Roxi Bahar Hewertson.—1 Edition.
      pages cm
   ISBN 978-0-07-183302-8 (hardback : alk. paper)—ISBN 0-07-183302-1 (alk. paper) 1. Leadership. I. Title.
   HD57.7.B343 2014
   658.4'092—dc23   2014019366

McGraw-Hill Education books are available at special quantity discounts to use as premiums and sales promotions or for use in corporate training programs. To contact a representative, please visit the Contact Us pages at www.mhprofessional.com.

To George, for his remarkable patience
and unconditional love.

Contents

Acknowledgments

It is only because of decades of learning, teaching, and working with people whom I love and respect that I was able to pull the many threads of a tapestry together to create this book. I hope that in some way, my contributions will add to the body of leadership knowledge for those who want and need it.

I deeply appreciate the ideas, inspiration, theories, books, models, trust, patience, critical thinking, support, feedback, and hard work of so many of my friends, family, authors, colleagues, clients, and partners, and the many smart and caring people who have helped me to understand what really matters. I am so grateful for those in my family who have gone before me and on whose shoulders I am proud to stand: my grandfather, Malek O'Shoara Bahar; my father, Hushang Bahar; and my aunt, Parvaneh Bahar, each of them a powerful visionary leader, author, and amazing human being.

This book would never have seen the light of day without my remarkable agent, Leticia Gomez. Her optimism and faith in this book kept me believing, and her talent brought it home. Casie Vogel, my first editor at McGraw-Hill, enthusiastically opened the door and welcomed me. And finally, Knox Huston, my new editor, made it all come beautifully together. Thank you one and all!

There are several people whom I simply must embarrass here. These are people who have fundamentally turned me inside out, shaken me up, and helped me become the person I am today. Rod Napier, my brilliant and trusted mentor, teacher, friend, butt kicker, cheerleader, and the wisest sage I've ever known, taught me how to dig deep, reach far, and trust my instincts. Hal Craft, the best leader anyone could ever hope for, a wise, strong, and graceful soul who trusted me, laughed with me, put up with my numerous moments of weirdness, and opened up a world of learning and achievement that changed my life forever. Professor Lee Dyer, my master's degree sponsor, mentor, advisor, and champion. All grad students should be so fortunate! Rich McDaniel, always my friend, who so often has helped me see that there was light when I was in the dark. My best friends, Ellen Foulkes and Barb Kathan, who have put up with me for months at a time—I thank you for being patient and continuing to text me, e-mail me, and send me pictures proving that there actually is life outside my office window. Jenn Kaye, my coach, and dear friend, who flew into town just to help me rearrange my brain cells! And last, but far from least, my brilliant, beautiful daughters, Lara and Jenna, who keep teaching me everything there is to know about the beauty, joy, and challenges of leading and loving at home. I thank you for all the gifts you give me every day by being the magical, strong, loving women you have become. I am so very lucky to be your mother!

Introduction

The game of life is like a boomerang. Our thoughts, deeds and words return to us sooner or later, with astounding accuracy.
—Florence Shinn

Fact 1: People are messy. Groups are messy. These truths are never going to change.

Fact 2: We all know what good and bad leadership looks like and feels like. These truths are unlikely to change.

Fact 3: Today, we continue to have a few great leaders, some pretty good leaders, and bucket loads of people in positions of authority who are mediocre, incompetent, or worse at leadership. These truths can change.

If you doubt Fact 3 even a little, consider the mismanagement, lack of leadership, corruption, pain, suffering, and financial disasters that failed leadership has caused in Lehman Brothers, British Petroleum, the U.S. Congress, Syria, AIG, Enron, WorldCom, Fannie Mae, J.P. Morgan, the Catholic Church, Penn State . . . the list goes on and on, with new revelations about failed leadership every day, in every walk of life, with a trail of tears following each one.

You would not let a surgeon operate without her proving that she had the necessary skill set to preserve human life. Yet, even though we know that leaders have a significant impact on people's lives and well-being, we allow them to operate in their sphere of influence without having to prove that they have the skill set or the integrity to lead anyone anywhere. Naming a star player as the new coach of the rest of the players is an act of madness unless that player has the leadership skill set and attitude needed to make that switch. When it works, it is often by luck, not by design. This does not make any kind of good business or common sense.

We need a revolutionary approach to today's global leadership crisis because business as usual is not working and will no longer address the needs of our world. We all deserve far better than what we have gotten for hundreds, if not thousands, of years in our businesses, houses of worship, higher education, governments, public schools, healthcare—really, everywhere. We need a new norm and culture within leadership that says, "If you are going to lead other people and mess around in their lives, you must first prove that you have the skill set to perform that essential part of your job well."

Let's take a quick look at reality. Here is a sampling of what has been reported about today's workplace and workforce. In a recent Development Dimensions International (DDI) global study, "Driving Workplace Performance Through High-Quality Conversations: What Leaders Must Do Every Day to Be Effective," DDI assessed thousands of senior and frontline leaders over 10 years based on observations of actual leadership behaviors. The 2013 study validates how important Emotional Intelligence competencies, particularly self-awareness and social skills, are in human interactions. Here is a sampling of the eye-popping results.[1]

- Only 11 percent of senior executives and 10 percent of frontline leaders are effective in conveying performance expectations and facilitating clear agreement on next steps.
- Only 10 percent of senior executives are highly effective at inviting ideas from others, and only a paltry 7 percent do a good job of gaining others' commitment.
- Only 6 percent of frontline leaders are highly effective in asking questions and facilitating involvement, and only 11 percent do a good job of demonstrating interpersonal diplomacy.
- Only 24 percent of frontline leaders are highly effective in responding to cues for maintaining others' self-esteem, and only 38 percent demonstrated empathy.
- Only 5 percent of senior executives are highly effective in disclosing and sharing their thoughts and feelings with others, one of the most powerful methods of building trust.

A large 2012 Manpower Survey said that a whopping 65 percent of employees are dissatisfied at work.[2]

In June 2013, the results of a comprehensive study of 150,000 full- and part-time workers during 2012 from Gallup's "State of the American Workplace Report"[3] were reported in the *New York Daily News*[4] and *Today*

Money.[5] The Gallup report tells us that workplace morale is horrible, with a shocking 70 percent of Americans feeling negative about their jobs. For a deeper understanding of the economic impact of these findings, I highly recommend reading the entire Gallup report. Here are just a few highlights cited:

- Only 30 percent of employees are engaged and inspired at work.
- About 52 percent of employees are present, but not engaged.
- A full 18 percent are actively disengaged or worse.
- As much as $550 billion in productivity is lost because of that 18 percent of actively disengaged employees.

These are compelling reasons why we need to *lead like it matters . . . because it does*! No kidding; no fooling.

You or someone close to you has probably been affected by an ineffective or even toxic leader. You may have observed or experienced a highly dysfunctional work culture. I'm going to assume, because you are reading this book, that you want to become or remain a member of the minority of "highly effective leaders" that I hope will some day become the majority!

There is no question in my mind that you are really good at a lot of things. It is also a safe bet that you have some gaps in your leadership skills that you could and should address. Am I right? Do you know what they are? It's all right. We all have gaps—we are human.

No matter where you are in your leadership journey today, this handbook of proven (over decades of testing and practice) and practical everyday "how to" tools and skills can be applied to raise your bar significantly, measurably, and consistently.

I am your tour guide; *you* are driving the bus. I have excellent maps. Your job is to read them and then personalize each one. Just as in any venture, your intrinsic motivation will have a direct impact on your success, plain and simple.

For a long time I called this book *The Ripple Effect*. I began by thinking about the age-old pastime of skipping stones across a pond. Each time a stone hits the water, the impact causes a ripple, and then a circular motion fans out, changing the body of water. Depending on the skill of the "skipper," a few or many new ripples are created. Regardless of the skipper's skill, there is at least one "kerplunk" and one set of ripples.

This playful activity teaches us, at a young age and in a subtle way, one of the most important lessons of leadership: that action has impact. As in nature, leaders' behaviors have a significant impact on their teams, their organizations, their families, and the world we work and live in every day. I often sum it up this way: a leader's behavior creates an impact similar to that of a pebble (or boulder) landing on a pond. Everything within the pond reacts to the impact. The ripples grow and spread until they reach the boundaries of their influence. So it goes with leaders, regardless of their intent.

There's more. When I observed those ripples more carefully, I noticed that they eventually returned to their place of origin. As in nature, the ripples (good or not so good) we create will come back to us, sooner or later. It follows, then, that it is in our best interest to get this thing called leadership as right as possible.

Learning how to generate a positive ripple effect must be a top priority for anyone who accepts a leadership role and wishes to succeed. In 35 years of leading, coaching, and teaching, I have not met even one person who wanted to be ineffective, incompetent, or unsuccessful. No one has ever said, "Roxi, please tell me how to lower morale and make my staff disengage and become more discontented." Not one single person has retained me to help him create a toxic culture in his organization. And never once has anyone asked me to help her lower productivity and profitability.

Of course, the opposite is true. People want to lead well; they care about making a positive difference within their sphere of influence or "pond," no matter where they work. People want to succeed. More often than not, they just don't know how.

It's not so much what leadership *is* that matters; it's what leaders *do* that matters.

There are a lot of books on the shelves that talk about what good or great leadership and management is and is not. There are excellent theories, models, and studies, some of which I will share with you. But it is often difficult, if not impossible, to figure out how to integrate all that good information and apply it to your work and your life. Sadly, there is very little practical help on how to actually *do* the day-to-day job of leading other people. Most of us are not CEOs of huge Fortune 500 corporations. They have access to all the leadership training and development resources that anyone could ever want. Whether they take advantage of those opportunities or not is a different question.

My goal is to help fill that gap so that you can navigate the challenges that arise every day in leadership more successfully. This is the primary reason that I wrote this book and continue to teach my courses.

There is also one more reason.

I would like you to help me *go out of business!* I am dead serious. Nothing would make me happier than to wake up tomorrow morning and discover that no one needed my help, coaching, advice, or intervention—because that would mean that every leader everywhere was putting into practice the advice and tools that he or she needed to lead well. Imagine what a different world it would be!

In the meantime, within these pages, you will find, in very practical terms, the tools you need to liberate and empower the leader within you.

Much of what you will read here about leading well, I have learned from my mentors, teachers, direct reports, bosses, clients, and students. After decades of practice and study, I am very clear about what works and what does not work. It has become my life's purpose to share what I know. Along the way, I've tripped into and over many epiphanies, even been smacked upside the head by them! Let's begin with eight "aha" leadership insights that have helped shape my understanding of the challenges that leaders face. While some of these may seem obvious, some may surprise you. I will explain each of them in Part 1.

Insight 1:   Knowing is the easy part. Doing is the hard part.
Insight 2:   Leading people is messy!
Insight 3:   Leadership is a *discipline*, not an accident.
Insight 4:   Leading and Individual Contribution require opposite skill sets and motivations.
Insight 5:   Leading is all about relationships!
Insight 6:   Learning the "soft skills" is hard!
Insight 7:   Most change efforts fail, and they don't have to.
Insight 8:   Leaders create and destroy cultures.

Then we'll move on to the *four core masteries* in which every leader needs to attain reasonable competence. These masteries will address all eight insights and more.

Personal Mastery. This is discovering who you are as a leader: your Emotional Intelligence; your style and preferences; your life purpose, values, and vision; and how you can and do impact others. This mastery will help you take an authentic look at yourself, past, present, and future. Here we will look at your leadership style, your intent versus your impact, how you arrived in the life and work where you are today, and finally, what really matters to you.

Interpersonal Mastery. This is discovering how you communicate and interact with others. We will work on several dialogue skills. These difficult "soft skills" are essential to successful leadership. We will focus on how to deeply listen, provide important and constructive feedback, and manage and transform conflicts.

Team Mastery. This is discovering how your team works and how its members work together and with you. We will focus on building teams from the ground up and/or maintaining high-functioning teams. We will discover the nature and power of group dynamics, decision making that works, delegation for development, and meetings that produce great results. You will get tools that will help you facilitate productive activities to increase team success.

Culture and Systems Mastery. This is discovering how your system and your organizational culture operate. Since you and your team affect others and others affect you, we will look closely at what is happening in your culture, including a cultural assessment tool I call the C.A.T. Scan. We will explore what can happen inside systems that will blow them up or make them stronger. We'll look at a cure for fragile cultures and focus on how to successfully lead change in your system, while ensuring accountability for results. Finally, we will gain an understanding of the nature of courage for yourself, and how to measure it in yourself, your teams, and your organization.

After decades of helping leaders with many similar challenges, my goal with this book is to focus on those areas that cause the most angst and pain for the most people, regardless of their industry or job title. While we cover more than the 10 skills I am listing here, these are the skill areas with which leaders seem to have the most difficulty. If all we do together is help you to be more effective with even one, two, or three of these, you will see an immediate return on your investment of time, energy, and the price of this book!

Here are 10 "how to" skills you will have in your new toolbox when you finish this book:

- Leverage your strengths and mitigate gaps in your style and skill set.
- Create a compelling and effective mission, vision, and set of values for yourself and your team.
- Cut wasteful meetings out of your life and lead effective, productive ones.
- Create constructive dialogues, including managing up and delegation.
- Facilitate effective team building.
- Decide how to decide with confidence.
- Prevent conflicts and/or address them quickly and gracefully.
- Learn how to assess your culture.
- Lead change initiatives that are not dead on arrival.
- Engage your employees and increase productivity and accountability.

All the exercises and activities we will do together are intended to help you save time, not lose it or waste it. Learning is already part of what you do every day. Do you read the paper, watch the news, or attend workshops, seminars, or conferences? Do you read instructions on how to put together a special menu, a bookshelf, or something else? Of course you do. Going through this process, you should find that you are working smarter, not harder, and you will be more confident and joyful at work.

The whole idea is to make it simple. Notice that I did not say easy. Becoming a great or even reasonably effective leader is a *lot* of work. Knowing who you are, what motivates you, and where your passions lie are essential—if you want to be excited about going to work and feeling successful.

Wherever you are right now on the leadership continuum is perfect, really it is! It does not matter how much or how little you know. Some chapters may cover things that you already know and do very well, some will be timely reminders, and some may be huge "aha" moments for you. You are the best judge of where you need to spend the most time.

It is essential that you are completely honest with yourself, or the whole process will be useless and a waste of your time. Remember, no one is watching! No one will know what you think or say to yourself unless you choose to share. This is a golden opportunity to really take a close look and to discover the truth about you as a leader.

Believe it or not, you may even decide after all is said and done, that you do not want to be a leader of other people. For some, that can be a really smart decision. I've taught courses where an individual had that realization, and it may have saved his life. The extreme stress of being someone whom you do not want to be and doing something that you do not want to do can be a killer, literally!

My job is to give you the right information and the right tools for this journey. Your job is to use what you need to get where you want to go. By the time we have completed the four masteries, you will have a valuable collection of practical tools in your toolbox and a handy reference guide in case you need a refresher or want to share an exercise with your team. I hope you dog-ear and highlight everything that you want to remember, and make a right mess out of this book. Then you will know you got the most out of it.

How to Use This Book

We start with you. Then we move on to examine your interpersonal success with others, including your team. Finally, we complete the picture by exploring the culture and the system in which you work. Individual Leader –> Team –> System, in that order.

The most effective way to use this book is to get yourself a notebook in which to write notes to yourself, work on the dozens of exercises, and answer questions as we go through each chapter. Because each chapter builds upon the one before it, it is best to make the trip through the book in the order in which the chapters and exercises appear rather than skipping around. After your first reading, skip around all you like. Mark the pages and chapters that you would like to revisit.

If you would like to check out my online leadership resources, just go to www.AskRoxi.com. You'll find free chapters of the course, a quick leadership style assessment, and access to my monthly newsletters. I want to thank you for picking up my book. To that end, you will receive *50 percent off the course price* if you would like to enroll in my online leadership course. Just click on the "Buy Now" page, select "Leading with Impact," and when prompted enter in your special *coupon code* exactly like this—*askroxileader*. In the meantime, I hope you enjoy the book.

Are you ready? Good—then let's get started!

Lead Like It Matters...

Because It Does

PART 1

THE EIGHT LEADERSHIP INSIGHTS

Chapter 1

WHAT ARE THE EIGHT LEADERSHIP INSIGHTS?

INSIGHT 1: KNOWING IS THE EASY PART. DOING IS THE HARD PART

We are what we repeatedly do. Excellence, then, is not an act, but a habit.
—ARISTOTLE

This is intended to be your leadership workbook, playbook, and handbook to help you get on with the doing part. All the rest of the insights are driven by Insight 1.

Some of the best intended and least effective leaders I have known have read and could easily quote dozens of books and even more articles on leadership. They often know the buzzwords and the jargon, the latest trend in strategic planning, and the newest way to build an organizational chart.

Evaluating and retaining this plethora of information in your brain is one thing. Integrating what you learn into your behaviors and actions and making it real for you and for those you lead is a much bigger challenge. Why? Because changing our behaviors is one of the most difficult feats known to humankind. There will be days when you might think it would be easier to jump across the Grand Canyon! Unlike jumping the Grand Canyon, changing behaviors *is* possible.

To do anything new or difficult, you must be truly motivated, and you must know exactly what you want to change. You need to identify what success looks like for you—not someone else's definition, but your definition. You also need to develop an ongoing focus, along with built-in, reliable sources of feedback about your progress.

For example, if you wanted to lose or gain 20 pounds, you would need a scale and/or clothing of a different size to provide you with a "feedback loop" that would let you know how much or how little progress you were making. It's the same with any goal, and certainly with any behavior change. You need to determine the right metrics, and you need to ensure that you are receiving feedback on your progress.

Once you combine knowing and doing, you are well on your way. Don't give up on something that matters to you. You can expect to slip and fall. You will screw up. I don't know anyone who rode a bike perfectly the first time. As you are learning and doing, be gentle with yourself. Don't expect perfection. Celebrate your progress because each step, no matter how small, gets you closer to your goal.

Insight 2: Leading People Is Messy!

I will pay more for the ability to deal with people than
for any other talent under the sun.
—John D. Rockefeller

When we accept the role, assignment, or "mantle" of leadership, it is important that we know what we're really getting into. People are, and will always be, unpredictable. There is no "plain vanilla" workplace or workforce. Each person is unique, and that means that leading people is complex, fun, interesting, frustrating, and, yes, messy.

Life happens, and it's full of triumphs and tragedies, any of which can happen to any one of us at any time. We can't predict surprises! The human emotions that show up at work can be confusing and disturbing to leaders. What if someone cries in my office? What if someone is threatening or screaming? What if someone is constantly telling jokes about someone else? And so on. Personalities, motivations, and styles are all over the map. Leaders have to be ready for just about anything and everything.

Like it or not, and believe it or not, all people, unless they are suffering from true brain anomalies, bring their emotions to work. People are 24-hour thinking-feeling creatures. They can and often do behave differently from our preconceived perceptions and/or assumptions about them. Our values drive our decisions, which generate emotions that often show up in our behaviors. It's a kneebone connected to the thighbone kind of thing!

Emotions, both happy and unhappy, are contagious and can spread like wildfire. Anyone who has been around several babies in the same room will have noticed that when the first baby begins to cry, most if not all of the other babies, one by one, will begin to whimper. This reaction doesn't disappear when we become adults. We still catch flyby emotions more quickly than we catch a cold.

No matter how much some people think that "feelings" are supposed to be kept out of the workplace, emotions leak out—from men and women, young and old, contained or gregarious. The idea that we can keep feelings out of the workplace is a lot of bunk. Besides, we *want* people to feel when it suits us, right? We want them to be loyal, grateful, ethical, engaged, and nice to the people they work with and for. These are all feeling-based behaviors. It's just the inconvenient feelings that we would like people to leave at the door. Sorry! It doesn't work that way. We all bring our 24-hour, lifelong selves into work, like it or not.

We know that some people can compartmentalize their emotional lives more neatly than others. However, if you can read body language well, you will see that the emotions are still there, just well hidden. In my experience, no matter how far under the surface those emotions are, sooner or later they will manifest themselves.

Leading is one of the most rewarding jobs anyone can have, if and only if leading is *joyful* for you. Yes, I said *joyful*, and I meant it. If you find that most of the time, you dread the messiness of leading people, please put this book down and go out there and do something that you really enjoy. Don't try to lead people unless you have a passion for it. You'll make yourself sick and everyone else at work and at home miserable. The human and business costs are far too high, and really—it's just not worth it.

INSIGHT 3: LEADERSHIP IS A *DISCIPLINE*, NOT AN ACCIDENT

All great achievements require time.
—MAYA ANGELOU

Those of you who already lead people (as opposed to technology, science, or thought leaders, for example) may think you got to your position because you are a good leader and were recognized as such. "They hired me, didn't they?" The sad truth is that you, along with the rest of us, probably got your first and even subsequent leadership roles by luck, not by design—and sometimes even by default.

If you are not a leader yet, but you feel that leading may be your calling, you should keep reading to make sure you know what you are getting into and to see whether leading is a good fit for you. Leaders find themselves responsible for the work lives of other people because their knowledge, performance, and technical skills as an individual contributor were exemplary, or at least pretty good. That doesn't mean that the whiz kid knows how to *lead* other whiz kids.

Learning to become an Olympic athlete, an engineer, a teacher, a scientist, or an opera singer requires one to learn increasingly difficult skills; to practice, practice, practice; and to receive regular feedback on one's performance again and again. This is also true for becoming, practicing, and remaining a skilled, effective leader.

Leading is both an art and a science, and it takes a lot of determination, skill, and practice to do it well. From an early age, we are taught how to follow, and even how to play well with others, but rarely, if ever, do we have the opportunity to learn the actual discipline of leadership.

Being an effective leader is not a title and requires more than mastering the ability to wield power and influence others. Stephen Covey told us about seven and then eight different habits. Jim Collins wrote an entire book about the differences between great and good leaders and their organizations; Daniel Goleman explained the art and the science of human Emotional Intelligence. And so it goes.

Leadership effectiveness can be accurately measured. We know for sure that highly effective leaders get much better results. There really is no debate about this, and in any case, it's plain old common sense. Don't we all want better results? Don't we all want to get more bang for the buck?

In colleges and universities around the globe, they often say "we are educating the future leaders of our world," and yet most college graduates leave school with years of course work under their belts, and without a single course in leadership. At one university I know well, students cannot graduate without learning how to swim. This fact made me wonder, though, what would happen if a bunch of swimmers were in a sinking ship? Would they simply swim their hearts out to reach safety on their own, or would any of them be able and willing to lead others (maybe even nonswimmers) to safety? When we examine leadership in higher education (and I have), it is abundantly clear that we are not training our young people in the discipline of leadership. Too often, we are not even hiring great leaders to lead our educational institutions. People move from professor to chair to dean to provost to president, but they are rarely, if ever, evaluated on their leadership ability or effectiveness. The same is true in our public school system, often in our businesses, our nonprofits, and definitely in our government. There is no fail safe litmus test to prove that one can lead effectively the way there is to prove that one can play Beethoven on the piano with finesse or serve a tennis ball. This moves us nicely into Insight 4.

INSIGHT 4: LEADING AND INDIVIDUAL CONTRIBUTION REQUIRE *OPPOSITE* SKILL SETS AND MOTIVATIONS

A leader's role is to raise people's aspirations for what they can become and to release their energies so they will try to get there.
—DAVID GERGEN

From the day we were born, all the applause has been about "what *I* have done well," not "what *we* have done well." Look at your life and your experiences and then fast-forward to where you are today. I think you'll agree that for most of your life, your personal performance generated the lion's share of your positive rewards or negative consequences. It wasn't a group of people; it was you, you, and more you.

The exception is teamwork within or outside your family. If you have been a member of a real team of any kind, you may have picked up some insight into the way teams work and even into the way good leadership works. Whether you were on a great team or a lousy team, you learned something about leading and teams. Unfortunately, few people integrate those lessons when they become leaders at work. The fallback position for most of us is what we know best and can count on the most—and that is *me*.

The skills and attributes required to lead people successfully are entirely *opposite* from the skills and attributes required to be a successful individual contributor.[1] The work, rewards, and impact are 180 degrees from each other. Consider this: if the roles and skills weren't so opposite, it would be a walk in the park for someone to move seamlessly from being a great violin player to being a great conductor. Knowing how to play one instrument flawlessly requires one skill set. Knowing how to create harmony from a symphony of people playing many varied instruments requires additional, different, and opposite skill sets. In the first case, the violin player is responsible for his performance. The conductor is responsible for knowing what the violin player is capable of and is meant to do, *and* understanding the job of every other performer in the orchestra. It is also the conductor's job to get the most out of each person and his or her instrument so that everyone will blend well together to produce magnificent music. While the soloists may be appreciated, the audience will remember the performance as a whole. The leader is responsible for the quality of the results. She and they succeed only when the entire orchestra succeeds.

For some people, this transition in roles may come more easily; for most of us, however, it's not a seamless shift because we have not learned how we can most effectively lead others to do their best work. We tend to come at leadership as though it were no big deal: "Hey, I'll get the hang of it—it's just like falling off a log." Or we may consider leading as just another line on our job description, equal or even subordinate to all the other duties and responsibilities listed there. The supervisor role is slapped on, and suddenly you find you still have most, if not all, of your old job and now you are expected to help others create good results. There might be time cards to approve, vacation schedules, health issues, and messy interpersonal conflicts to deal with, all without getting much, if any, information about how to manage any of those new responsibilities gracefully. Talk about setting up people to fail! This is rarely intentional, and nevertheless, it happens far too often.

Leading others is an emotional and intellectual seismic shift that will quickly separate effective leaders from ineffective ones. Making the transition from being an individual contributor to being a leader can seem as difficult as swimming from New York to London alone, without a life jacket.

After reading and working with this book, I hope you will feel that you are not alone, that you have a lifeboat as well as a life jacket and at least one friend cheering you on.

How can you make the leadership leap gracefully, you might ask. Of course I'm going to tell you to read my book and do every exercise in it at least once, if not multiple times! Here are some other suggestions: take a really good leadership development course, find a willing and seasoned mentor who is a good leader, observe other good leaders around you to see how they behave and what they do, observe bad or mediocre leaders around you, and finally, regularly ask for and listen carefully to constructive feedback from your direct reports, your stakeholders, your peers, and your boss.

Get out of the weeds and *lead*. When you have your entire team fired up and producing great results, you can be far more strategic, including ensuring a sustainable future for your "pond." At long last, there will be time and space for you to be proactive rather than reactive. When you get it right, you will be amazed at how much more time you have to think, to create, and to have fun at work. This is not a wild theory, an empty promise, or even wishful thinking. It's real—and it's a beautiful thing.

Insight 5: Leading Is *All* About Relationships!

> *A major reason capable people fail to advance is that they don't work well with their colleagues.*
> —Lee Iacocca

Let's get to the heart of the matter. If no one is following you, you aren't leading. You can manage tasks, schedules, money, projects, budgets, and spreadsheets. Managing people well means *leading* them where they didn't know they could go. You can do that only if you have good working relationships, and, of course, that requires respect and trust.

No matter what I'm doing (coaching, teaching, or facilitating), I say this to everyone: "It's all about relationships." There are few, if any, people around the world who want to or are able to live and work entirely alone. Even those who are self-employed and/or who work on their own must interact with other human beings in order to get paid, eat, have shelter and clothing, move from one place to another, and so on. That deep human connection reflects our basic primal and tribal needs. We believe that without one another, we will die. We believe this because it is true. There may be wars, famines, earthquakes, tsunamis, genocide, disease, and other such situations in which we die either because of one another or because of nature, but unless we manage to wipe out the entire human species, we will keep finding ways to utilize our combined skills to survive and thrive. Humans have done this for tens of thousands of years. I think it's safe to assume that we won't lose our drive to survive any time soon.

The question is not *if* we will have relationships at work; the question is what the quality of those relationships will be. Leaders must understand the critical part they play in the ecosystem that they affect and the well-being of what I fondly call our "responsibility pond." This is where our leadership ripples are most strongly felt.

When you are a leader, you create, model, and nurture (on purpose or not) the norms, culture, and environment for everyone in your "tribe." You will sustain and strengthen them, or you will weaken, sicken, and even kill them. Understanding this reality is a huge wake-up call for many leaders, and in my opinion, not a minute too soon.

We are not alone. I'm not talking about UFOs; I'm talking about the fact that we are all connected in ways that we are aware of, many ways that we take for granted, and even more ways that we are not aware of. Not only do we need one another, but we have a dramatic impact on one another's well-being, emotionally, physically, intellectually, and spiritually. There is no escaping this.

I've already mentioned that emotions are contagious. We don't need dozens of research papers to tell us that. Just as yawning and laughter catch on, so do optimism, creativity, a "can-do" attitude, and trust. The flip side is also true. Doubt, negativity, fear, and anger are highly contagious.

When you are leading, you must pay attention to which emotional virus is rolling around your pond. Is it healthy or sick? Did you start the epidemic or contribute to it? Do you have the antidote to cure it if needed? As (Leroy) Eldridge Cleaver said, "You're either part of the solution or part of the problem." When you are the leader, you need to be part of the solution.

Of course, emotions aren't the only things that are affecting your pond. Physical, mental, and spiritual energy is floating around in there, too. It's quite a soup. When we explore culture, we'll look at the impact of relationships and culture on the whole system.

Remember, this is your ecosystem, and you need to be smart about what happens there. To lead others well, you must understand yourself and how best to communicate, negotiate, and work well with others. You need to know how to build your team, facilitate progress, and manage conflicts. It is also your job to know how to work within the system in which you and your team need to swim. Emotional Intelligence matters when you lead. It's not enough for a leader to be really, really smart intellectually. You need to have so much more going on in that brain of yours—and in that heart of yours.

Everything and everyone in your pond is connected. It is, in fact, organic and alive, and therefore it is affected by both internal and external forces. If you choose to lead, you need to know what's happening to your pond and all the life within it. You also need to be aware of how your pond is affecting other ecosystems within the larger system—you know, the one that provides your paycheck.

Leading well is clearly a big deal. It shapes lives, companies, communities, countries, and our world. Bad leaders can do a lot of damage. Good leaders can heal the damage done by others as well as accomplish incredible feats with their followers. I believe most of us would choose the latter as our legacy.

When I am coaching leaders, I always ask them why they want to lead and whether they enjoy it. To those who have any trouble at all answering, I say this: "Leading and being an individual contributor are both valuable and honorable roles in life and at work. If you enjoy the job of leading people, and you have been given the opportunity to do that job, make time to learn how to do it the best you can. If you really don't like the job of leading people, stop doing it. This choice *really matters*, so choose wisely and choose well."

Insight 6: Learning the "Soft Skills" Is Hard!

No company, small or large, can win over the long run without energized employees who believe in the mission and understand how to achieve it.
—Jack Welch

Adults often tend to resist learning or relearning good interpersonal and social management skills. These skills involve thinking about relationships, behaviors, and even emotions rather than just the impersonal task at hand.

And this *is* hard work. Yet every leader wants high productivity and great results. Well-informed leaders know that they need to engage and energize employees, build trust, and communicate so that people understand where the organization is going and what part everyone needs to play in getting there. We can't get all that good stuff without doing all the hard "soft" stuff. It's that simple.

Bad habits are hard to break. Failing to build good habits is a very big, shortsighted mistake. Mastering leadership skills is *not* rocket science—it's a *lot* harder, precisely because it is more qualitative than quantitative, and because we are leading people, not machines.

For all this hard work, you'll want and need a leadership workbook, playbook, and handbook. How lucky for you that you happen to have all three in front of you!

As a *workbook*, this book provides essential practice in the "soft skills" arena. Dialogue skills—truly listening, giving constructive feedback, and conflict resolution and transformation—are the three major skills in this area that we will cover in the book. Building trust is one of the key outcomes of mastering these interpersonal skills. Try to control your urge to say, "Oh, no—not the touchy-feely stuff." Let's get all your sighing out of the way now so that we can move on, and you can move up in confidence and competence. Besides, it's just you and me here, so who will know how you got so leaderly smart? They will just be glad you did, right?

I want to reassure you that although it takes determination, practice, and feedback, nothing in this book is beyond you, and most of it will not even surprise you. Yet, as Stephen Covey observed (and I wholeheartedly agree), "What's common sense just isn't common practice." I wrote this book to help you integrate commonsense leadership practices into your real work with real people.

The *playbook* will include terrific handy-dandy materials that you can play with. You can practice and utilize many of these activities with your teams and direct reports in building and enhancing successful relationships and teams. The tools I am giving you are ones that I use in my own practice, so I am positive that they work. Don't worry, I will coach you through each of them. You can skip the things that you know *and* do well now, and focus only on the things that you need to know.

The *handbook* means that wherever you go, you can carry this book around in your briefcase, book reader, handbag, or knapsack. You'll be able to look up whatever you need for that meeting or conversation, just in time! You will have your very own coach right there in your pocket!

I am not implying that everything you ever wanted to know about leadership can be found in this book, or that I'm providing a solution to every situation you encounter. It does mean, though, that most of the time, most of the things that you need to understand and practice as a leader of people are in here. You might be looking for a tool, a method, an activity, or a message that you can use and share to suit the situation at hand. We don't need 100 percent solutions as leaders. I'm happy to shoot for the Pareto principle of 80/20.[2]

INSIGHT 7: MOST CHANGE EFFORTS FAIL, AND THEY DON'T HAVE TO

The things we fear most in organizations—fluctuations, disturbances, inbalances—are the primary sources of creativity.
—MARGARET J. WHEATLEY

Think of the wasted human energy and wasted capital, human and financial, that go down the big black sinkhole of most change initiatives. It's astounding. Do we learn from our mistakes? Usually not a lot, and nearly always, not enough.

Leaders lead change—there's no getting around it. How you do that part of your job will make or break your organization and probably you. A colleague once told me that he loved it when I said, "I eat change for breakfast." I didn't even realize I had said that. What I really meant to say was, "I love change. I thrive on change, and it energizes me—as long as it's *my* change and I have control!"

The painful truth is, change efforts fail about 70 percent of the time.[3,4]

Instinctively we know this, although there are those who argue that it's not scientifically quantifiable, so we shouldn't say 70 percent. It doesn't really matter what the exact percentage is, does it? What matters is that it is very high; we all know this from our own experiences.

The status quo has a powerful, almost surreal stranglehold on people and organizations. We think and say that we are open to new ideas and change, but it's often not true. Why? In part because our life experience tells us that people in leadership roles often make lousy decisions based on lousy information that have lousy results. That's why.

The number one reason that change efforts fail is people. When something is going to change your work life, you tend to care a lot about it, and if you are not involved in making the change, you generally will not react very well, sometimes even when the change is positive. Fortunately, there are smart ways to lead change initiatives that go well and actually stick. We will cover resistance, responses, and leading successful change together, and I will give you tools that you can actually use.

INSIGHT 8: LEADERS CREATE AND DESTROY CULTURES

If you are lucky enough to be someone's employer, then you have a moral obligation to make sure people do look forward to coming to work in the morning.
—JOHN MACKEY

Leaders have responsibility for the culture, period. Your number one role is to create, model, and support a workplace environment in which the intended culture will thrive and the desired results will occur.

I learned this the hard way—the really hard way. I spent more than a decade of my life building a collaborative culture with my colleagues, four unions, and a professional and support staff of nearly 2,000 people. We were all immensely proud of what we accomplished together. Trust was high; fear was low. Creativity and innovation were rampant. Productivity skyrocketed. Bottom lines got healthier; we faced only one lawsuit in 10 years, and we won; there were few arbitrations, and we lost none of them. The leadership was getting stronger and stronger at all levels. This was a slam-dunk dollars-and-cents return on investment (ROI) that we could prove to anyone! There was no question about the value to the larger organization of our success in building a healthy values-based culture.

I had a dream job in a dream culture that I had helped create. But it didn't last after us. As our senior leadership team was getting older and older, I knew that we should be paying a lot more attention to the future. I remember ringing the warning bell a number of times; it must not have been at the right decibel level. Half of us retired or left to pursue other dreams within a couple of years of one another, and our hard-won culture began to unravel, one leader at a time. That's when I truly realized there is much more to leading right than leading right—in the moment.

The Native Peoples had a great philosophy. They considered seven generations beyond themselves when they made their decisions. "What must we do to ensure that seven generations from today, our people will still survive and thrive?"

I would have been happy if our leadership team had been thinking seven *years* down the road! We weren't, though, and today, 10 years later, almost nothing of the organization or culture that we built is still visible. We saw a dramatic change in leadership at the top, and a diminished core at the next level. There was nothing and no one strong enough to prevent the destruction of our culture.

When a strong leader is the main or only cultural "glue" and that leader leaves, the culture often leaves with him. Fools rush in. It happens all the time; just look around and you'll see it everywhere.

It takes years of hard work by everyone involved to build and sustain a positive and productive work culture. It takes a "heartbeat" for one ineffective, bad, or lousy senior leader to destroy it. We need a solution to this insane and vicious cycle, one that goes beyond a good succession plan. I'll share my discovery with you when we talk about culture and systems mastery. It's part of the leadership paradigm revolution that I hope to see happen in my lifetime.

There you have it, my eight leadership insights. Of course, there are more insights woven into this fascinating tapestry of leadership. I've saved them to discuss with you in various chapters as we take this journey together. We'll dive in, one core mastery at a time, until you have unwrapped and tucked away everything you need.

PART 2

PERSONAL MASTERY

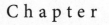

WHAT IS PERSONAL MASTERY?

If you don't understand yourself, you don't understand anybody else.
—NIKKI GIOVANNI

Instead of waiting for a leader you can believe in, try this: become a leader you can believe in.
—STAN SLAP

WHAT IS PERSONAL MASTERY?

Definition: "Personal mastery is the discipline of continually clarifying and deepening our personal vision, of focusing our energies, of developing patience, and of seeing reality objectively. And it goes beyond competence and skills, although it involves them. People with a high level of personal mastery live in a continual learning mode. They never "arrive." Personal mastery is not something you possess. It is a process. It is a lifelong discipline."—PETER SENGE[1]

We will first create some context for personal mastery. Then we will explore Emotional Intelligence, a key differentiator between leaders who succeed and those who don't. We will take a look at personal preferences and style through the lens of the Myers-Briggs Type Indicator. We will take a step back in time to look at themes and patterns that you've encountered in your life's journey up through today, using your own Life Line. Finally, we will help you understand how your personal values, mission, and vision affect who you are and how you lead.

The study of leadership began at least as early as Plato, Socrates, and other early philosophers. Down through the ages have come the great stories about heroes and heroines, their journeys, and powerful archetypes of right and wrong, good and evil, impact versus intent. Every culture tells similar underlying stories over and over again through ceremony and ritual, dance, music, traditions, movies, novels, television shows, and so on.

Storytelling is one of our first and most enduring social behaviors. We have a deeply rooted fascination with the actions and behaviors of other people, particularly leaders, and the impact that those leaders have on our lives, and for good reason. They matter to us.

Leaders are present in every aspect of our lives. They are our parents, leading in the home; religious leaders influencing their worshipers; government leaders affecting the fates of thousands or millions; business leaders driving our economy; educational leaders touching young minds; bosses in any space and place; informal leaders; coaches; team captains; volunteers in the community; gang leaders; and so on. They bring light or darkness into our lives and provide positive or negative models that we may even carry to our graves.

There is an enormous body of knowledge and opinion about leadership. The last time I typed the word *leadership* into a search engine on the Internet, it returned 136 million results in just under half a second. Everyone seems to have an opinion about what is and what isn't good leadership. And yet, you and I both know a good leader when we experience her. We also know a lousy or downright horrible leader when we see one, and we know it early on. No one has to give us a book or a course to teach us this. We learn these lessons as children, and we don't forget them.

I've tracked the responses of literally thousands of people who have answered this question for me: "What are the qualities, skills, and competencies you want in your leaders?" I'd like you to guess what you think is the number one answer time and time again. Is it "smart" or "knowledgeable" or "technically competent," or maybe "experienced"?

Not even close. The number one answer is: "Cares about her people and shows it." Bundled into that big category are usually things like "trustworthy," "walks the talk," "inspires us," "compassionate," "listens," "communicates vision," and the like. All of these are directly related to demonstrating Emotional Intelligence competencies, as we'll see in a bit.

How the leader interacts, develops, and engages with his people shows up in about 85 percent of the answers. Yes, the "what" also matters. It is important that the leader be able to demonstrate the necessary knowledge and have good technical skills in his area of expertise. Leaders do need to be competent in the business side of their jobs. However, all these competencies together get about 15 percent of the votes. Why? Because most people believe that the necessary knowledge, experience, and technical competencies are a given, that the "hard" technical skills got the person's ticket punched before he could even get in the door. The rest—well, the rest has to be earned.

This is common sense, right? Yet, in every line of work—profit, non-profit, government, schools—we still today, in the twenty-first century, hire and promote leaders based primarily on their technical skills rather than their leadership acumen. Is it any wonder that we have a crisis in leadership today?

Coming up is Exercise 1. You will have exercises like this all the way through the book to help you answer questions for yourself, gain more awareness, and practice various skills and tools. I suggested earlier on that you get yourself a notebook to write in. Now is the time to start using it.

In Exercise 1, you will identify three leaders who mattered to you. You know and can feel how much those leaders' actions and behaviors affected you. Well, you can be certain that if other leaders' actions and behaviors affected you, your actions and behaviors matter a heck of a lot to those you lead. For at least some of them, you are what others have been for you—a leader who matters.

Exercise 1
Three Leaders Who Mattered to You

Think of three leaders who have had a *big impact* on your life, for good or for ill. Remember their faces, remember their voices, and consider how you feel about each leader's impact on you and why. They could be parents, teachers, mentors, coaches, bosses, someone you read or heard about, someone in a movie that you saw, or someone else. You know who they are.

Use your notebook now to write down your answers. I'd like you to get quite specific about each leader's direct or even indirect impact on you and your life.

Who are they?   Name 1   Name 2   Name 3
In how many ways did each of these leaders affect your life?
How do you feel about each of them and why?

Take the time you need to answer these three questions fully before reading on.

Exercise 2
Intent versus Impact

Please take out your notebook again. This time, answer these four questions:

1. When was the last time you absolutely knew that your intention and your impact *did not* match at home or at work?
2. How could you tell?
3. What did you do about it?
4. What happened next?

Every leader's actions result, sooner or later, in equal or opposite reactions. The reasons that this is true are complex and sometimes unpredictable, but the truth of this becomes abundantly clear when we take the time to observe group dynamics and leaders over time.

Remember our "pond"? Every drop of water, every molecule, and every submicron particle in the pond *is* the pond. All drops are connected, and when anything affects any part of the pond, all of the pond is affected. The ripple effect of one person's choices and decisions can be profound, even in the most limited exchange.

You need to become mindful of your impact on other people because:

- You have a ripple effect on others.
- When we can see others, we can see ourselves, and when we can see ourselves, we can see others.
- Leaders often mean well, but their words and actions may not come across to the receiver the way they intended.
- When your intentions and your impact do not match, you can recover—an apology never killed anyone!
- You can learn and use deep listening, constructive feedback, and conflict management skills to help you.

Chapter 3

EMOTIONAL INTELLIGENCE AND PERSONAL MASTERY

There is no separation of mind and emotions; emotions, thinking, and learning are all linked.
—ERIC JENSEN

WHAT IS EMOTIONAL INTELLIGENCE?

Definition: Emotional Intelligence is the capacity for recognizing our own feelings and those of others, for motivating ourselves, and for managing emotions in ourselves and in others.[1]

Daniel Goleman, in his first book on the subject, talks about the most essential of the emotions, "self-awareness—the ability to read your own emotions and gage your moods accurately, and know how they are affecting others." Awareness is only part of the equation, however. We need to be skilled enough or intuitive enough to control our emotions honestly and with integrity. Goleman calls this "self-management." None of this happens without context; we have to be "socially aware" and tuned in to our environment and the people in our lives, their emotions, and their realities. What makes us effective in our interactions with others is how skilled we are in "relationship management," or the ability to communicate clearly and convincingly, deal with conflicts, provide constructive feedback, request feedback, and manage situations and people with finesse.[2]

This may seem like a tall order, especially for those of us who have been socialized and rewarded for "taking charge," "kicking butt and taking names," "making it happen," "playing nice," "not rocking the boat," or any combination of the messages from parents, bosses, media, and social interactions of all kinds that we have on our internal tapes.

If you would like to fully understand Emotional Intelligence (EI) or Emotional Quotient (EQ), terms that are used interchangeably today, I highly recommend that you read both *Emotional Intelligence* and *Primal Leadership*[3] from cover to cover. I am a certified practitioner with the EI instrumentation, and teach the material in my courses. It's included here because I am 100 percent positive that to be an effective leader, you need to incorporate and practice all of the Emotional Intelligence competencies. Besides, if you don't understand yourself, you won't get far with personal mastery.

Human beings have an enormous capacity to learn, change, adapt, and improve. We have the unique ability within the animal kingdom to make reasoned and emotional choices, and we are capable of communicating all that to others.

We cannot control how others choose to internalize our behaviors and actions, but we do need to be aware that they are doing so. We must recognize our impact and then consciously choose what parts of it we want to have start, stop, or continue because the outcomes of our impact will keep showing up.

We can run from ourselves, but we cannot hide.

Personal responsibility is at the core of personal mastery. In fact, no matter how clever we think we are at "hiding" ourselves from others, we don't—in fact, we can't (unless, of course, we are classic sociopaths). We telegraph our real thoughts and feelings through our faces, bodies, tone of voice, and actions. Not everyone can read them well, but most of us can read a lot more than even we realize.

The ripples just keep coming.

To make well-informed choices about which habits, behaviors, and attitudes we want to "keep" and which we are ready to "let go," we first need to understand how we got here. We didn't land on this planet fully formed, with dozens of years of experience, traumas, knowledge, joys, wisdom, neuroses, and so on. We did land here with a personality, a gender, and a family of some sort, and we grew into ourselves over time. All of this has affected who we are and how we "do" ourselves.

We can get ourselves unstuck from self-defeating patterns and become more aware. We can become more authentic by growing our personal mastery skills. Let's start with an understanding of our own Emotional Intelligence.

A lot of smart people fail at leadership because:

- IQ, knowledge, and technical expertise are threshold capabilities, not differentiators for success.
- EI is twice as important as IQ *and* technical expertise combined.
- EI is four times as important in terms of overall success.
- EI is *the* differentiating factor; 90 percent of the difference between outstanding and average leaders is linked to EI.
- Only *one* cognitive ability, that of pattern recognition, differentiates outstanding leaders.

Since top professionals are typically in the top 10 percent on intelligence, IQ itself offers relatively little competitive advantage. And yet we hire, reward, and promote people based on their cognitive and technical abilities first and their Emotional Intelligence second, if we consider it at all.

EI is simply about:

- Understanding yourself
- Managing yourself
- Understanding others
- Managing others

The really good news is that Emotional Intelligence is developed from emotional competencies that are and can be learned capabilities and that contribute to effective work performance, outstanding leadership, and deeply satisfying relationships in life.

A competency is any measurable characteristic of a person that differentiates his level of performance in a given job, role, organization, or culture. Within Emotional Intelligence, there are four quadrants with 12 specific competencies that are necessary if someone is to be a highly effective leader.

Let's look at each one. As you read through these, be honest with yourself. Give yourself a high, medium, or low score on each competency to reflect how well you believe you demonstrate this competency.

SELF-AWARENESS

Emotional self-awareness means recognizing how your emotions affect your performance. People who demonstrate this competency know the signals that tell them what they're feeling, and use those signals as an ongoing guide to how they are doing in life. Recognizing how your emotions affect your performance has a significant impact on those around you.

SELF-MANAGEMENT

Achievement orientation measures how much you are striving to meet or exceed a standard of excellence that you and/or others have set for you. People who demonstrate this competency look for ways to do things better, set challenging goals, and take calculated risks.

Adaptability focuses on your flexibility in handling change. People who demonstrate this competency willingly change their own ideas or approaches based on new information or changing needs. They are able to juggle multiple demands. Innovation and changes in the status quo are generally seen as opportunities, not things to be avoided.

Emotional self-control involves keeping disruptive emotions and impulses in check. Since we all have these impulses from time to time, people who demonstrate this competency are able to maintain their effectiveness under stressful or hostile conditions.

Positive outlook focuses on persistence in pursuing goals despite obstacles and setbacks. People who demonstrate this will see the positive in people, situations, and events more often than the negative. They tend to have an abundant attitude toward life rather than an attitude of scarcity.

SOCIAL AWARENESS

Empathy is sensing others' feelings and perspectives, and taking an active interest in their concerns. It's paying attention and being "tuned in." People who demonstrate this competency are able to pick up cues, understand what others are feeling and thinking, and can truly "walk a mile in someone else's shoes" even if they have not had a similar experience.

Organizational awareness focuses on the dynamics among people. It is about reading a group's emotional currents and understanding the power relationships among its members. People who demonstrate this competency think about the interconnectedness of relationships throughout the organization, not just their part of it. They can accurately identify the influencers, the networks, and the group dynamics.

Relationship Management

Conflict management measures how well you negotiate and resolve conflict. People who demonstrate this competency bring disagreements into the open, communicate the different positions effectively, and find solutions everyone can endorse. They do not allow unresolved conflicts to create or sustain a dysfunctional environment.

Coach and mentor means taking an active interest in others' development needs and bolstering their abilities. People who demonstrate this competency spend time helping people via feedback, support, and assignments that will grow their skills and capabilities.

Influence means having a positive impact on others. People who demonstrate this competency can persuade or convince others to gain support for an agenda. They are able to use their insights and their awareness of others' needs to get other people on board with a change, a new idea, or a plan of action.

Inspirational leadership means the ability to inspire and guide individuals and groups. People who demonstrate this competency work to bring people together to get the job done. They bring out the best in others, and people love to follow an inspirational leader to places where they didn't know they could go.

Teamwork requires working with others toward a shared goal and creating group synergy and group identity in pursuing collective goals. Teamwork is an orientation toward working with others interdependently, not separately or competitively. Leaders with this competency understand that the whole is far greater than the sum of the parts when the whole is working well together.

Now it's time for you to take a quick self-inventory. I created this short inventory from my many years of working with clients and asking many of these Emotional Intelligence competency questions. It is a brief indicator that will help you identify areas you may want to explore as well as areas where you are consistently strong. Answer in the book or use your notebook. You will need to be really honest with yourself if this exercise is to be helpful.

Exercise 3
Emotional Intelligence Quick Self-Inventory

Score yourself on a scale of 1 to 5, where
1 = Very Rarely and 5 = Very Consistently

1._____   I know how I'm feeling.
2._____   I know and share my strengths and weaknesses.
3._____   I address conflicts before they get out of hand.
4._____   I keep calm in a crisis or when I'm under stress.
5._____   I don't let unexpected events throw me for long.
6._____   I see the positive more than the negative in people and situations.
7._____   I actively seek others' perspectives and opinions.
8._____   I do a good job of "walking a mile in someone's shoes."
9._____   I know how to work with and through others in my organization.
10._____   I understand how our culture works here.
11._____   I provide constructive feedback to those who need the information.
12._____   I ask for constructive feedback about my impact on others.
13._____   I understand how different people need to hear or see information.
14._____   I enjoy encouraging excitement and inspiration in others.
15._____   I know why I'm feeling the way I am.
16._____   I set goals for myself that are realistic and challenging.
17._____   I know what my triggers are.
18._____   I look for ways to improve the way things are.
19._____   I look for subtle signs in the way people are communicating.
20._____   I make a conscious effort to engage every member of my team.

Transfer your scores to the Self-Inventory Scoring Grid

Exercise 3
Emotional Intelligence Quick Self-Inventory Scoring Grid

Transfer your self-score for each question number from the 20 questions sheet, and then total your score by adding up the scores on all the questions for each of the four EI quadrants.

Self-Awareness	Self-Management	Social Awareness	Relationship Mgmt
1.	4.	7.	3.
2.	5.	8.	11.
12.	6.	9.	13.
15.	16.	10.	14.
17.	18.	19.	20.
Total:	Total:	Total:	Total:

The maximum score for each quadrant is 25.

Those quadrants with the higher scores are those in which you probably have the most awareness and EI competency. Those with the lower scores are those in which you probably need to focus more of your time and effort. Also pay attention to specific high or low question scores to enhance or focus your learning and practice.

This Quick Self-Inventory has not been scientifically validated. It is drawn from the hundreds of questions that EI-certified trainers and coaches ask their clients. It is only a brief indicator of the EI areas that you may wish to explore further.

Tony was one of the brightest young leaders I'd ever met, chock full of energy and great ideas. At only 28, he had been promoted to be director of an IT department with more than 50 people and a multimillion-dollar budget. The group's work had a dramatic impact on the entire organization and its more than 25,000 people. Tony's IQ was very high. His technical knowledge was extraordinary. *But* . . . his EI/EQ was microscopic, with a 1 or a 2 on most questions. Tony was in deep trouble as a leader. I was asked to intervene to try to "save" him. His people loathed him (no exaggeration!), occasionally even going so far as to sabotage his projects. Tony needed data and lots of it before he could even entertain the idea that he was the one, rather than "my lazy employees," who had a problem. I gave him data that he could not deny—so much so that his normal talkative self became very quiet. When it finally sunk in how much he had damaged his people, his relationships with them, and the work they were trying to do, he was devastated. To his credit, he called an all-hands meeting, completely owned his mistakes, genuinely apologized, and asked them to help him become the leader they deserved. There wasn't a dry eye in the house, including mine! His people agreed to give Tony another chance to lead.

Fortunately, Emotional Intelligence can be learned. In fact, many of the exercises I've included throughout this book are specifically designed to help you do just that, no matter how much or how little EI you have learned and integrated into your life before now.

Speaking of learning, it occurs in a predictable pattern that you will recognize, I'm sure. There are four phases that take us from not knowing something to being highly competent at a skill or area of expertise.

1. *Unconscious incompetence* (not as bad as it sounds!). This simply means, "I don't know what I don't know." Habits and autopilot responses fall into this category. Another way to think about it is to remember when you were a kid, before you even knew that bicycles existed. You didn't know you didn't know about them, and you certainly couldn't ride one.
2. *Conscious incompetence*. This means, "I know that I don't know." We discover this through the feedback we get from life experience and/or from people. At this point, you *know* that there are bicycles because you saw a person riding one, and you know you haven't mastered

that skill yet. This is a *decision point* for you. Do you want to become competent at riding a bike (learning a skill)? If so, you will need to practice until you reach the third step.

3. *Conscious competence.* This means that you now know how to ride a bike. You experimented; you fell down, scratched your knees, and got up and did it all over again until you became pretty good at riding a bike. When you reach this stage, there's another decision point: how competent do you want to become? If you want to race your bicycle in a competition, this requires Step 4. You will need to become unconsciously competent.

4. *Unconsciously competent.* This happens when you have practiced, experienced, and learned enough for highly skilled bike riding to be fully integrated into your being—in other words, you can "do it in your sleep." The skill is part of you, who you are, and how you operate in life. That doesn't mean you can stop paying attention to the state of your bike, your health, or which competitions you enter. It means that when you are on that bike, riding in the wind, it just flows, and you are in your realm of expertise.

Take a look at the EI learning model given in Figure 3.1 to help you visualize what you have just read. Consider your scores in the EI self-inventory. Pick one area where you scored yourself 3 or below and walk yourself through the learning model.

As you can see, your decisions and choices are going to drive your competence at anything you put your mind to. A self-directed change and learning process may begin at any point in a person's life and often begins when that person experiences a discrepancy or an event that evokes a new awareness and a sense of urgency.

Self-directed action planning is exactly what you are doing by reading this book and doing the exercises. As you go through the book, it will help you to:

- Determine the best model of leadership for yourself—what kind of a leader do you want to be? What style?
- Ensure that you receive ongoing feedback, and identify the areas where you want to develop and grow.
- Evaluate the feedback and internalize what matters to you.
- Create your action plan and monitor progress on your action plan.
- Be mindful, be aware, and practice, practice, and more practice!

Figure 3.1   Learning Model

Conscious Incompetence I <u>know</u> I don't know. I can choose to learn this skill and learn more by asking for and receiving: **Feedback** **2**	**Conscious Competence** I know. I can get better at this skill by: **Experimentation** **3**
Unconscious Incompetence I <u>don't know</u> what I don't know. This is a result of forming a: **Habit** **1**	**Unconscious Competence** I can do this in my sleep. This is a result of experiencing and knowing enough for full: **Integration** **4**

To learn a lot more about your perceived leadership competencies impact, I recommend using a validated 360-degree feedback instrument. It will give you an accurate view of how you are perceived as a leader, usually including your boss, direct reports, peers, and others who can provide you with constructive feedback. It's called 360-degree feedback because you ask people for data and they return their answers full circle to you. Rodney Napier, PhD, was the first person I know who used the term "360-degree feedback." He developed a measurement tool for leaders in the 1980s. He doesn't get the credit he deserves, so I'm giving it to him here.

Here is a warning: you must never use a 360-degree feedback instrument to measure your own or others' performance; use it only for development, and never try to discover who said what. If you ignore these fundamental tenets, your data has a high probability of being contaminated from the outset and will likely prevent you from receiving honest information in the future. Instead of being a great tool and helpful to you, the results can be toxic. When the instrument is used for developmental purposes, the overall results are highly reliable.

Any well-tested and validated instrument that measures leadership competencies will align with Emotional Intelligence competencies in a number of ways because you can't lead well without them. There is an excellent instrument that you can use online at www.AskRoxi.com. It has been researched and validated thoroughly, and I have successfully used it with many of my clients. I recommend that you work with someone you trust to help you understand and integrate the data you receive.

Chapter 4

MYERS-BRIGGS TYPE INDICATOR

Everything that irritates us about others can lead us to an
understanding of ourselves.
—CARL JUNG

The Myers-Briggs Type Indicator (MBTI) is just that: an indicator. It is not a test, nor is it like reading your horoscope, and no one's personality type is "better" than anyone else's. It is an instrument that has been researched and validated for more than six decades. The MBTI sorts; it does not measure or evaluate. If you wish to learn the ins and outs and history of the MBTI, there is a plethora of information on the web, in books, in doctoral dissertations, and in many other resources. CPP, Inc., holds the license for the MBTI instrumentation, administering the reports and certifying practitioners (https://www.cpp.com/en/index.aspx). I use the MBTI as a very useful tool in helping people understand themselves and others better.

You might think of personality preference as being a lot like hand preference. We are born with a preference for right or left-handedness. Unless we are forced to behave differently, we are going to prefer one hand over the other for most things. Yet, as you know, if you were to injure your preferred hand, your other hand would still work. I'd like you to try something now.

Exercise 4
Write Your Name

Please take out a pen and paper. I would like you to write your name four times.

1. With your eyes open, write your name as you normally do with your preferred hand.
2. With your eyes closed, write your name with your preferred hand.
3. With your eyes open, write your name with the opposite hand.
4. With your eyes closed, write your name with the opposite hand.

How did that feel? I expect that the first time you wrote your name, you were in your comfort zone, right? It was a bit awkward when you lost one of your senses, sight, but you still did pretty well. It was probably more awkward using the hand that you rarely use to write. And finally, the most awkward and uncomfortable of all was both having your eyes closed and using the "wrong" hand. And yet, you could do all four, and with practice, you would get better and better at it.

That's how it goes with personality preference. The father of preference, Carl Jung, believed that we are "hard-wired" at birth; I don't know whether we pop into the world fully loaded with our personalities or not, but I expect this is at least partially accurate. For instance, parents of identical twins can immediately point out the differences in personality in their "identical" newborns.

Jung also pointed out that we can and do develop the capacity to broaden our understanding of ourselves and others—to nuance our responses to life as we mature, get more comfortable in our own skin, and learn what works well and doesn't work well for us in our relationships. That's where I'd like to focus your attention. Because, with practice, we can all access each dichotomy within the MBTI. It's important to learn what is working for you and where you might *stretch*. I'm going to briefly summarize each dichotomy first, and then provide more detail so that you can get a good sense of your own personality within the MBTI.

Figure 4.1 shows the four dichotomies in the MBTI. Two are attitudes, and these are generally more visible to the world. The other two are internal processes or functions.

Figure 4.1   The Four Dichotomies

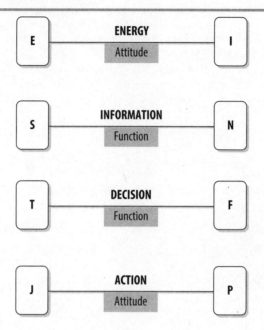

The first is *energy*. We receive and regenerate our energy either externally (extraversion) or internally (introversion).

The second is *information*. This is how we make sense of our world. We take in all kinds of stimuli from the world we live in and sort them to figure out what we are experiencing. In doing this, we put more trust in either our five senses (seeing, hearing, tasting, smelling, and touching) or our intuition.

The third is *decision*. Our preference is either to be logical and objective thinkers or to be more focused on people, relationships, and feelings.

The fourth is *action*. Either we prefer order and control to help us make things happen in an organized way, or we prefer to be more adaptive, open-ended, and spontaneous.

Within each of these dichotomies are nuanced layers of factors that, with the appropriate instrument, can help you interpret your results in more detail. If you wish to explore this further, you can contact CPP at custserv@cpp.com to be directed to a certified practitioner.

There is a range of clarity of preferences from very clear to slight. The nuances definitely affect our behaviors. For our purposes here, I would like you to simply appreciate that people have very different personalities and that their "normal" is whoever *they* are, not who *you* are.

EXTRAVERT AND INTROVERT

This is all about energy. It reflects whether you receive most of your energy from the outer world of people and objects and experiences, Extraversion (E), or from your inner world of thoughts, concepts, and internal experiences, Introversion (I).

Extraversion	Introversion
Outside focus	Inner focus
Talks to think	Thinks to talk
Involved with people and things	Works with ideas and thoughts
Interaction	Reflection
Do-think-do	Think-do-think

Where Are You? ___

SENSING AND INTUITION

This dichotomy reflects your preferred way of sorting information and perceiving or making sense of the world, either through your five senses, Sensing (S), or through understanding the world through processes beyond the conscious mind, iNtuition (N). Since the *I* was used for Introversion, *N* gets the call here!

Sensing	iNtuition
Facts and details	Big picture and vision
Present and past orientation	Future orientation
What *IS*?	What *IF*?
Practical	Inspirational
Concrete	Theoretical
Perfecting established skills	Learning new skills
Learns step by step	Learns insight by insight
Understands the world using the five senses	Sixth sense, gut hunch

Where Are You? ___

THINKING AND FEELING

This dichotomy reflects your preferred way of making a decision: either through a logical, objective, and impersonal process, Thinking (T), or through a decision based on personal and social values, Feeling (F). Of course, Thinkers feel and Feelers think. Where you land, at the end of the day, tells you what you prefer in making decisions.

Thinking	Feeling
Logic	Value system
Head	Heart
Objective	Subjective
Justice/Balance	Mercy/Fairness
Critique	Empathy
Principles	No one size fits all
Reason	Compassion
Firm but fair	Harmony

Where Are You? __

JUDGING AND PERCEIVING

This dichotomy identifies the preference used to interact with the outside world and take action. The word *Judging* does not mean being judgmental, and the dichotomy doesn't mean that Judgers can't perceive or that Perceivers make no judgments. This is all about the way you act on your decisions—with a preference either for order and control or for letting life happen and flow.

Judging	Perceiving
Decide about information	Attend to and gather information
Control	Flow
Settled	Adapt
Run one's life	Let life happen
Close off ideas	Open-ended
Organized	Tentative
Structured	Spontaneous
Follow the plan	Seek options, flexible

Where Are You? __

You can get a better idea of your preferences by doing two things. First, answer the four questions in Exercise 5. You can also get a good idea with the free Jung Typology Report online at www.humanmetrics.com. It only takes a few minutes and it's fun! Even without the deeper detail, this will get you started.

Exercise 5
Four MBTI Questions for *You*

Please take out your notebook and answer these four questions.

1. If you were planning an ideal, no-work weekend where you had full control over the people, activities, and location, what would your ideal weekend look like?
2. Please describe the chair you are sitting in.
3. Please tell me how you prefer to receive performance feedback from your leader.
4. Imagine this: you've just been handed an envelope telling you that you've received an all-expenses-paid two-week trip to Hawaii for you and, if you like, your immediate family. The only snag is that you have to leave in two days or you will lose it completely. Please make a list of the things you would do to get ready to go on this trip.

In the first question, if you want a lot of people, activities, noise, fun, and variety, Extraversion is more likely your preference. If you want an intimate, small group of friends and family at home or in a comfortable place where you can have quiet, good conversation, your preference is more likely to be Introversion.

In the second question, if you described your chair mostly by its physical qualities, such as size, material, color, fabric, and the like, you probably prefer Sensing. If you described it in terms of how you use it or its meaning to you, like it's a place to rest, it's an old favorite from your grandmother, or sometimes it's your stepstool, you are likely to prefer iNtuition.

In the third question, if you said, "Give it to me straight; don't beat around the bush," and you want the good, the bad, and the ugly without a lot of fluff, you probably prefer Thinking. If you prefer a boss who delivers this information in a kind, compassionate, and personal way, you are more likely to prefer Feeling.

In the fourth question, if you said, "Oh, no! That's a *lot* of pressure to get everything on my list done in two days—can I have more time?" then you are probably going to prefer Judging. If you said something like, "I'll tell my boss, give the dog to my mother to watch, and then get on that plane," Perceiving is probably your preference.

It's important to remember that the MBTI shines a light on only one part of who we are. Please, do not stereotype yourself or others! The MBTI does not touch upon your values, your education, your cognitive intelligence, your Emotional Intelligence, your abilities, your talents, your traumas, your birth order, how far you can stretch yourself, or anything else. It's *only* about your personality preferences—and it really can help explain why we keep running into the same buzz saw with another person and wondering whether we might prefer working with someone who has a more compatible personality.

Dan was promoted to the executive director job when his predecessor retired. In many ways, his personality was opposite to that of his longtime boss. They had balanced each other well. But now Dan was in charge, and there was no one balancing him in the same way. After a year on the job, Dan wanted to take a deep temperature check to see how he was doing. I interviewed all his direct reports and some of his key board members, administered the MBTI, and conducted a 360-degree feedback process. When all this was complete, I provided him with his instrumentation and a summary report of the interviews. I told him, and it was 100 percent true, that I'd never met a leader who was so well balanced, so well loved, and so well respected by all his followers. Dan was happy and relieved by the news. He told me that he had worked very hard for many years to stretch his ESTJ personality to have more access to introversion, intuition, feeling, and perceiving, because he knew he wanted to be a well-rounded, accessible leader. He said it took work and attention, but he needed to keep at it in order to relate well to his 800 employees and the thousands of clients and their families served by the organization. I told Dan his leadership journey had paid off big time and asked for his permission to tell his story in my book. Obviously, he agreed, and he was very humble in doing so, thanking me, when really, I was thanking him for leading like it matters!

As with anything in life, overuse of a good thing can get us into trouble. So it goes with preferences. For example, too much extraversion can overpower people, and too little interaction can be seen as disinterest. Too much objectivity can seem uncaring and cold, while too much focus on harmony can make us avoid conflicts. Too much order can stifle people, and too many open ends can make people anxious and rudderless. It's all about balance: we get more balanced when we stretch as a leader and move out of our comfort zone to broaden our understanding and approach.

A good example of balance is the Z model of decision making (see Figure 4.2). Using what we know about the MBTI, this can help us make better decisions. By asking questions that focus on the four middle functions, sensing, intuition, thinking, and feeling, we will get a broader and deeper understanding. We will get the facts and details from the sensor perspective and consider the possibilities from the intuitive perspective. We will pay attention to the impact on things by using our thinking function and the impact on people by using our feeling function.

Let's try it out. Perhaps you are considering buying a house. It's a good idea to get all the *facts* about price, age, repairs needed, and so on. It's good to know whether it's *possible* for you to add on to the house, or maybe put in a pool. You certainly need to figure out what the *impact on your budget will be*, and maybe your commute. Certainly it's important to consider how this purchase will *affect your happiness* and that of anyone who might live there with you—do you like the neighborhood; is it safe? Rather than considering only one or two of your favorite perspectives, make a list of the answers to each of these four MBTI functions before you make your decision.

Figure 4.2   Z Model of Decision Making

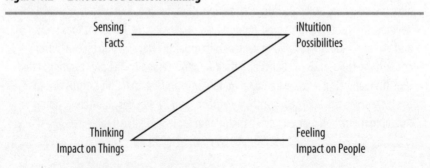

In the Z model, we ask four questions:

- What are the facts that we know or need to know about this question or decision?
- What are the possibilities that we should consider when making this decision?
- What are the impacts on things (budget, commute time, status, and so on)?
- What are the impacts on people (emotions, happiness, safety, and so on)?

Exercise 6
Using the Z Model to Help Make Decisions

Please take out your notebook and draw a big Z on the page.

- Consider a decision you need to make soon—the bigger the better.
- Walk yourself through the Z model, asking questions from each of the four perspectives.
- List as many answers as you can under each perspective—stretch yourself.
- Take a look at what you said. How many of these questions, perspectives, and insights would you have come up with normally?

If you don't have a decision pending, think about one that you made recently (a good one or a bad one) and walk yourself through the process to see what perspectives you included and what perspectives you left out.

Chapter 5

LIFE LINE

We don't receive wisdom; we must discover it for ourselves after a journey that no one can take for us or spare us.
—MARCEL PROUST

In personal mastery, we need to answer important questions about who we are, what really matters to us, and where we want to go. Even if you already think about these things from time to time, now is as good a time as any for you to stop, pause, and gather some insight in a structured way.

We are going to do a number of different exercises to help you figure all this out. The first one is called a Life Line.[1] It allows you to create a visual rendering of your life from your early years to the present. By the end of Part II, you'll know a lot more about yourself than you did when we started. And, of course, that gives you a lot more self-awareness—a core Emotional Intelligence competency.

The Life Line is a timeline of your life from three perspectives: personal, achievements (school and/or work), and other events.

Exercise 7
Creating Your Life Line

1. Take out your notebook and draw a vertical line down the left side of the paper and a horizontal line at the bottom from left to right (see the Life Line example in Figure 5.1).
2. Label the horizontal timeline with your age, beginning no later than eight years old and moving forward in time in five-year increments. Give yourself space for some years ahead of you.
3. The vertical line shows positive and negative impacts, with positive at the top and negative at the bottom.
4. Draw another horizontal line that cuts the chart in half so that you have as much space in the top half as you do in the bottom half and label it neutral.

Now for the three perspectives:

5. It helps to draw each perspective in a different color or design so that you know which is which.
6. The *first Life Line* on your chart records *personal events or people* that directly influenced your social and personal development. The focus is on relationship issues, which might include things like moving to a different house, loss of friends, being in a committed relationship, or having children.
7. The *second Life Line* records *achievements throughout your life*. These events can be either major successes or major failures, such as graduating from college or your first job disaster.
8. The *third Life Line* plots *other events* that don't fall neatly into the other two categories, but that had a profound impact on you. Perhaps an inheritance, a sudden insight, or a spiritual experience might fall into this category.
9. After you have completed this exercise—and it could be an emotional experience, I'd like you to note trends, spikes, dips, and patterns that you see on a single line AND in comparing lines. Try to identify several high and/or low points in each of the three categories.
10. Mark the key events, people, or situations in each category to help you focus on the main things that matter to you.

Figure 5.1   Life Line

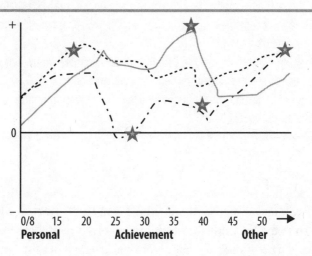

A completed Life Line might look something like the one in Figure 5.1. Yours will be whatever it is meant to be; it could even be circular. You don't have to follow the rules! You just need to find a way to create a picture of what's happened in your life to help you figure out where you want to go next on your journey. To get the most insight, take all the time you need to answer the questions in Exercise 8.

Exercise 8
Your Life Line Insights

Let's take a look at what you wrote down: the *highs*, the *lows*, and the *neutrals*. I'd like you to consider these five questions and write the answers in your notebook.

1. What was the impact of each of these important relationships, achievements, and events on your perspective on the world?
2. How do these relationships, achievements, and events affect the way you behave in the world today?

(Continued)

3. What "pains and triumphs" did you identify, and how have they influenced your life? Have you been able to let go of the pain? Are you able to acknowledge the triumphs and own them?
4. What are the patterns you see in your overall development on any one line and among the three lines? Where do you think you are headed?
5. What does all this tell you about how you lead, what you want most, and what you care most about?

It is often helpful for you to share your Life Line and your insights with someone who knows you well and whom you trust. Talking with another person also helps to bring the emotions involved in these experiences to the surface. Pay attention to that emotional energy—it's important, and it helps you zero in on the person and leader you want to become.

You have begun your personal mastery journey in earnest. We've established why the quality of your leadership matters. We now know why Emotional Intelligence is such a big deal and how we can increase it in ourselves. The MBTI is now part of your awareness and understanding, and finally, you've taken a walk down memory lane to gain insight into where you've come from and where you are headed.

Now it's time to explore your personal values, mission, and vision. Knowing (explicitly) these things about yourself can make everything in life much clearer and can make your choices about your life and your career a whole lot easier and more fun.

Chapter 6

PERSONAL VALUES

Happiness is when what you think, what you say,
and what you do are in harmony.
—MAHATMA GANDHI

Definition: Personal values are the beliefs and philosophies about life, its purpose, and how we should behave and act that we hold deeply. Our values are central to our sense of ourselves. Personal values are implicitly related to choice; they guide and even drive our decisions.

Values, therefore, are a big deal. We hear about them all the time: family values, company values, spiritual values, and so on.

As we grow, we take on board the personal values of others around us until we reach our teen years, when we start to accept or reject such values as being a part of who we are or who we want to be. They may be derived from the values of a particular group or system, such as a culture, a religion, or a political party. Personal values are not universal; one's family, experience, community, nation, culture, and historical environment influence one's personal values. Each individual has a unique conception of her own values as they apply to her life.

Some things in life are so fundamental, so ever-present, that we rarely even take the time to think about them. Yet, our personal values subtly or overtly influence every action or decision that we make, and they determine the nature of all our personal relationships. Clarifying our personal values requires taking a deeper look at ourselves and our assumptions. It is well worth the effort to know, rather than assume, what matters most to you. Every value that you hold translates into one or more behaviors that guide how you interact with others.

The workplace, too, has its values—the expectations, beliefs, or traditions of behavior that underlie most decisions and that, in the most fundamental way, determine the climate and culture of the workplace. When our personal values and our workplace values agree, there is resonance and productivity. When they disagree, the cognitive dissonance can be debilitating to both the individual and the organization.

Sometimes, an organization's *true values* are not stated explicitly. Members learn of them by trial and error and by following others' examples. The true values are those that people believe to be the case and use to determine how they operate, not what's written on the wall, in a handbook, or on a website.

For example, we all know of organizations that have valued profit and financial performance over everything else, but say, "People are our most important asset." In fact, they behave as though money is their most important asset, which means that it is. I've been in schools that say that children's learning matters more than anything else, but that behave as though adult rules and policies matter far more than children's emotions, learning, or experience.

Unless the leaders actually behave and make decisions in ways that show that the values they profess are true, their value statements become so much ink, and a painful lie in print. The reverse is also true. When values are alive and well throughout an organization, they bring clarity and accountability, and they help build a sense of community for the members of the group.

Shared values are the glue in any system, no matter how large or small, formal or informal. It doesn't matter whether the values are positive or negative, or whether the system is a corporation, a choir group, or a gang. People bond tightly around values they share and are important to them. Consider the influence that values have on members of the Ku Klux Klan, Al Qaida, and the Mafia or the members of MADD (Mothers Against Drunk Driving), Doctors Without Borders, and the Girl Scouts.

The norms or expected behaviors within a culture, and the values upon which they are based, are established, consciously or unconsciously (usually the latter), by the way the leaders of that organization behave and what they expect. Therefore, what leaders say certainly matters, but what they do matters far more to the individuals in the organization.

There is no way to hide those leadership values, and there is no way to blame others for them. This is the responsibility that comes with the mantle of leadership. The leader is accountable for the values that operate in his sphere of influence. Period.

Since your personal values are translated to the workplace, your values are your true motivators, and you make your decisions based on them, it is wise to make sure that you are keenly aware of what those values are and why they are important to you. You know what they are on some level, but people rarely take the time to really think about them, about how they may have changed over time, or about how widely they affect our lives. That's why we are going to explore your values here.

Identifying personal values is not necessarily easy. Exercise 9 can help by presenting a list of possible values that can guide our lives. Most of these will seem important to most people. The challenge is to identify those *few* that are intrinsically most important, rewarding, and inspiring to you. You want to identify those values that exemplify your strongest motivators, which are often your greatest source of joy when you are living them, and your greatest source of unease when you are not.

Milton Rokeach, in his book *The Nature of Human Values*,[1] says that there are two kinds of human values: instrumental and terminal values. Instrumental values involve ways of being that help us arrive at terminal values. For instance, you may have an instrumental value of "ambitious" that supports your terminal value of "family security," or an instrumental value of "imaginative" supporting a terminal value of "an exciting life." Terminal values are end states of feeling; they are the emotional state that you prefer experiencing. Terminal values, such as self-respect and happiness, make our life fulfilling and worthwhile; instrumental values help get us there.

I have provided a list of 36 values. You may add any that do not appear in the list and that matter to you. If you add a value, try to identify it as either instrumental or terminal. There are four parts to Exercise 9. Please go through each carefully.

I hope you identified your key drivers and the order in which they play out for you. You might find that there can be situations in which a couple of your values may be in conflict. For instance, I might say that I value freedom, but if my family's safety would be compromised or my family would starve if I suddenly quit my job just to be free, then one value would end up trumping the other. We do have a hierarchy and it may change, just as our values may change over time. It's a good idea to revisit your values from

Exercise 9a
Step 1: Choose Your Top 10—Mark with an X

Instrumental Values

1		Ambitious (hardworking, aspiring)
2		Broadminded (open-minded)
3		Capable (competent, effective)
4		Cheerful (lighthearted, joyful)
5		Clean (neat, tidy)
6		Courageous (standing up for your beliefs)
7		Forgiving (willing to pardon others)
8		Helpful (working for the welfare of others)
9		Honest (sincere, truthful)
10		Imaginative (daring, creative)
11		Independent (self-reliant, self-sufficient)
12		Intellectual (intelligent, reflective)
13		Logical (consistent, rational)
14		Loving (affectionate, tender)
15		Obedient (dutiful, respectful)
16		Polite (courteous, well-mannered)
17		Responsible (dependable, reliable)
18		Self-controlled (restrained, self-disciplined)

Terminal Values

19	A world at peace (free of war and conflict)
20	Family security (taking care of loved ones)
21	Freedom (independence, free choice)
22	Equality (brotherhood, equal opportunity for all)
23	Self-respect (self-esteem)
24	Happiness (contentedness)
25	Wisdom (a mature understanding of life)
26	National security (protection from attack)
27	Salvation (eternal life)
28	True friendship (close companionship)
29	A sense of accomplishment (a lasting contribution)
30	Inner harmony (freedom from inner conflict)
31	A comfortable life (a prosperous life)
32	Mature love (sexual and spiritual intimacy)
33	A world of beauty (beauty of nature and the arts)
34	Pleasure (an enjoyable, leisurely life)
35	Social recognition (respect, admiration)
36	An exciting life (a stimulating, active life)

If "Others," indicate whether they are (I) or (T): _____

Exercise 9b
Step 2: Choose Your Top 5 of the 10 and Define Them

Take out your notebook, list your top five values in any order, and write a definition beside each one. Example: *If a top value is* Responsible, *my definition might be, "I make sure I do what is needed, when it's needed."*

1. Value and your definition:

2. Value and your definition:

3. Value and your definition:

4. Value and your definition:

5. Value and your definition:

Exercise 9c
Step 3: Rank-Order Your Top Five and Consider Why

In your notebook, list each of your top five values in **rank order** and write a definition beside each one. Example: *If my top value is* Responsible, *my reasons for that might be that I have a deep need to live a life that affects others positively, and that I want to do an excellent job at whatever I do.*

Rank Order of Your Top Five Values

1.
2.
3.
4.
5.

Exercise 9d
Step 4: Test Each Value Against Your Real Decisions

Do you really make your decisions based on these values, and in that order? How closely does each of your values mirror your beliefs, words, and actions? If you are not sure, review your list again. No one else knows what you've decided, so please tell yourself the truth when you write your answers in your notebook.

Value   How does this value affect my behaviors, actions, and decisions?

1.
2.
3.
4.
5.

time to time to see what is driving you and motivating you, and to help you stay true to yourself.

Pay attention to the alignment of your personal values and those that exist in your workplace. When they are in harmony, all is probably well in your world; if they are not, then you'll need to decide what you want to do about it. Can you influence the workplace values so that they are better aligned with yours? Is a disconnect making you unhappy or even ill? I suggest that you give this some thought, because it affects everything you do and how you feel about your work and your workplace. It affects how you feel even when you are away from work. And when you are a leader, all those feelings will leak out to others in either good or not-so-good ways.

Alice had been working with and for foundations for about 10 years. After about a year of navigating several sticky situations, she believed that her foundation's values and her personal values were in serious conflict. When we examined all the issues thoroughly, it became clear that Alice had two competing personal values: personal financial security and professional fiscal responsibility at work. She was very concerned that she was going to have to decide which one was more important to her life and to her career. As we explored further, it became clear that the dissonance at work didn't violate her deeply held ethical values; it was a philosophical difference, not a values difference. She was able to reframe her job with that in mind and the dissonance disappeared.

Being very aware of how values are operating in your life will make you more self-aware and more able to manage your life. Like the earlier exercises, this also increases your Emotional Intelligence and helps you make better decisions.

Chapter 7

PERSONAL MISSION

*Your purpose in life is to find your purpose and give your
whole heart and soul to it.*
—GAUTAMA BUDDHA

Before we begin discovering your mission, I am going to give you a brief definition of the difference between a mission and a vision because people often confuse the two, whether they are doing this exercise for themselves, for a team, or for an organization.

Definition: Your mission is your purpose: what you do and maybe even why you do it, or perhaps what gives your life meaning. It's in the now, the present. You can explain it clearly and in a few words. Your vision, on the other hand, is your passionate dream for the future; it hasn't happened yet. We will create your vision after we complete our work on your mission.

There are four short steps in this exercise. You will need your notebook again.[1] While the steps are short, you need to give the exercise your full attention if you are to get where you need to go. You will get the most out of it when you really stop to think about the questions and feel the answers resonating within you.

Exercise 10a
Step 1: Personal Characteristics

List personal characteristics that you feel *great* about. These should be *nouns*. There is no maximum; the minimum is three.

Begin with the words: "I have . . . ," and then fill in your nouns.

Examples: *technical expertise, energy, creativity, sense of humor, courage . . .*

Exercise 10b
Step 2: Ways You Interact with People

List the many ways in which you successfully interact with other people. These should be *verbs*. There is no maximum; the minimum is three.

Begin with: "I . . . ," and then fill in your verbs.

Examples: *teach, lead, serve, support, inspire, collaborate, produce . . .*

Exercise 10c
Step 3: Visualize Your Ideal World

Visualize your *ideal* world—the one you would like to work and live in. What are the people in your ideal world doing and saying? Write a description of this ideal world. There is no word limit.

Begin with, "In my *ideal* world, . . ."

Example: *"Everyone, especially leaders, is awake to her authentic self and is being that person in the world, making it a much better place for all."*

Exercise 10d
Step 4: Bringing It All Together

Combine two of your *nouns* and two of your *verbs* with your definition of your *ideal world*.

Begin with, "My life purpose is . . ."

Example: *"to use my coaching and teaching skills to inspire and guide leaders to become their best authentic selves."*

The outcome of this exercise may have surprised you. It doesn't matter how you get clear on your mission—it matters only *that* you get clear. Otherwise you can become a ship without a rudder and get tossed about in the waves of life rather than being the captain of your own ship and your own journey. It is worth taking the time to keep at it until you hit on a purpose in life that resonates deeply within you.

Chapter 8

PERSONAL VISION

The future belongs to those who believe in the beauty of their dreams.
—ELEANOR ROOSEVELT

*To the person who does not know where he wants to go
there is no favorable wind.*
—SENECA

What is visioning, and why does it matter to you? *Definition: Your vision is your passionate dream for the future.* It is your picture of a purpose achieved; it is the fuel that fires your spirit and the spirits of those around you. It's something you can imagine that moves you and your life forward. It gives you hope. It is that which makes you refuse to get sidelined with doubts, such as "if only," "I wish," or "I can't see how." And finally, it is something that you have the courage to say, "make it so."

You are so busy doing, doing, and more doing, right? So why bother? Well, you cannot go very far as a leader without having a vision for yourself, your organization, or your team. Change is a constant in life, so you can let it all happen *to* you, or you can develop a vision of a future that you prefer and work toward that light.

What we can envision, we can realize. Everyone can do it. *You* have to make the time, and *you* have to make the choice.

Stuff—family, friends, work, e-mails, phone calls, TV—gets in the way, right? I know; I live in the same world as you. And I make time to develop a vision regularly because it's so important. This book *is* a vision realized.

Consider:

- What are *your* blocks to visioning?
- What happens when *you* don't have a vision? What do you lose? How does that feel?
- When was the last time you realized a vision for yourself and your life? How did that feel?

Here are some answers about blocks that I've heard frequently from people in my courses: "I have no time," "I don't know how," "I can't focus," "It's just daydreaming," "It didn't work last time," "I'm afraid of what I want," "I can't have what I want," and, sadly, "I don't deserve what I want." The reality is, we can let anything stop us from developing a vision, *or not*.

How you spend your time and use your mind *is* your choice.

When we don't have a vision, we stand still, lose hope, become pessimistic, stop growing, stop learning, and we are definitely not taking charge of our future. We can become victims of our own unwillingness to identify a vision.

Remember, anyone can vision. I'm going to show you how by giving you some exercises to help you get in a visioning frame of mind. If you haven't done this before or if you've done it only rarely, it may take you a few attempts before you can quiet your mind and allow yourself the time and the space. That's fine. Just do it and keep doing it.

You will need to set aside about 30 minutes to go through the two exercises. I highly recommend making more time available for serious quiet stretches to really give yourself the opportunity to hear what you need to hear and feel what you need to feel. Our world is so noisy that we can become numb; it takes conscious effort to make the quiet happen.

The first exercise is called Writing Down the Bones, inspired by the creative writing book of the same name by Natalie Goldberg.[1] We are going to use a technique that is used in creative writing to help you begin to liberate yourself from your left brain, your ego, and your internal critic so that you can think and feel in new ways, if you allow it.

There are four questions. You will need your notebook and a timer that alerts you when you have spent three minutes on each question. You should use a pencil or a free-flowing pen that moves easily on the page. There is a specific method for this exercise, so please trust me to walk you through it. Give yourself the chance to free up your thinking with no judgment.

Here are a few rules for Writing Down the Bones. These rules will set you free, and yet you will still resist them, so repeat them to yourself if you need to.

- Set your timer for three minutes.
- Write down your first thought, best thought.
- Keep your hand moving *at all times*, even if you can't think of anything to say; if necessary, write, "I can't think of anything," but keep writing.
- Don't cross out or erase.
- No computers. It's important to physically write on paper with a writing tool.
- Don't worry about punctuation, grammar, spelling, or handwriting.
- Lose control, do not edit yourself in any way—just keep writing.
- Don't evaluate your writing or get logical.
- Go for it! *Let loose!*

If you are ready with paper, pen or pencil, and your timer, and you are in a comfortable writing space, then let's begin. Seriously, do it with the timer; don't just look at the questions and answer them in your head. It doesn't work.

Exercise 11
Writing Down the Bones Four Questions

1. One year from now, I can teach others . . .

2. Ten years from now, I'm most proud of . . .

3. When my friends and family talk about me, they say . . .

4. The 27 things I want to do before I die are . . .

Good! Now read over what you wrote, slowly. Take your time. I'd like you to notice any patterns in your answers. Did you see a lot about family, work, or something else? What seems to matter most to you? On your list of 27 things you want to do before you die, I would like you to choose *at least two* of them to put into motion in the relatively near future. Make them happen for yourself.

You can certainly create different questions any time you like, and take as much as 10 or 20 minutes to write *nonstop*. Sooner or later, you will tell yourself what you need to hear.

With the second exercise, Guided Visualization,[2] I would normally talk you through this in person; since that is not an option here, I will help you experience this visualization on your own.

Guided visualization is not hypnosis or even formal meditation. You will have the opportunity to imagine a future for yourself in a very pleasant way. Remember, you can take yourself on or off this journey any time you wish to. In order to get past attitudes and real and perceived obstacles that sometimes make it hard for us to dream, it is helpful for us to take ourselves into the future and look backward.

I deeply believe in the power of visioning. In 2008, I attended an Art of Leadership workshop with Robert Gass, who so generously shared this particular visioning method with our group. I use a number of visioning methods with my clients, and they all work well; still, this one that Robert shared with us felt really powerful to me. I envisioned my community of nonprofit leaders modeling the best leadership skills as they guided their agencies. They were lifting others to new places and collaborating in new ways. This idea had never entered my mind before. In under three years, I was teaching my six-day leadership course to 25 of our community's nonprofit leaders—funded by those who believed in my vision—and I'll do it again this year. It all started with a single clear vision!

I'd like you to read through the process carefully before doing it. The second time you read it visualize yourself through it, and with your eyes closed, in a quiet, comfortable, private place, with absolutely no distractions to give you a jolt. Lie down if you like. Take off your shoes. Allow yourself to get quiet. I will suggest a series of images. Trust and work with whatever pictures, senses, feelings, and thoughts arise in response to the imagery.

In this brief guided journey, we will travel three years into the future, a future in which your vision has been realized. Remember, there is no one who can tell you what to think, how to think, or what to envision for yourself; that is your right, your choice, and your responsibility. Here we go!

Exercise 12
Guided Visualization

- Please make yourself very comfortable and quiet, and close your eyes.
- Take three very deep breaths. Relax and feel your body settle into your space. Keep breathing deeply as you continue.
- *Slowly*, relax your body to release all the tension and stress that you may be holding, beginning with your toes and moving up through your calves, hips, lower back, chest, neck and shoulders, head and facial muscles, neck and shoulders again, and finally your arms and hands, releasing any remaining tension or stress out through the ends of your fingers. Relax; breathe; relax; breathe.
- Now, I'd like you to travel to a safe, beautiful place in your mind. It is a sanctuary for you. Where is it? Why do you love it? When you arrive, look around with your mind's eye. Smell what you smell, hear what you hear, and drink in the surroundings in your sanctuary.
- This place is only for you—it's safe; it's beautiful; it's peaceful. Revel in this space as long as you like before we move on.

I would like you to notice . . .

- A blanket in your space and on it rests a desk calendar that shows only one day per page. Notice it says today's date. And slowly, you see the pages begin to turn, one by one. The days, weeks, and months seem to just float by page by page. You can almost sense the seasons passing. And now you notice it is exactly three years from today and the calendar has stopped moving. You know, absolutely know, that your vision has been realized. All those things that you worked for and your highest hopes have come to pass. It feels right; it is right; it's how you really want it to be—it's what you believe in. Take your time to really enjoy this moment.

(Continued)

- Now notice that there is a magazine you didn't see before. It is on the other side of the blanket—it is a magazine that is telling the story about YOUR vision.
- What magazine is it? Is it one you know or a new one related to your vision?
- What does the front cover look like?
- Turn to the article now—you can see it's all about your vision realized. Notice there are some words in **bold**—the main points of what has come to pass. What is the story saying about your vision? What are those main points? Read them to yourself.
- In the middle of the article, you see the word *breakthrough*. This is telling about the *breakthrough* that ensured your success. *What* does it say there?
- You also notice that there are photographs throughout the article. Who and what are in those photographs? Are you there? Are you smiling?
- Take it all in, and then breathe several deep breaths and let yourself feel what you feel.
- When you are ready to return to the room where you started, do so gently and open your eyes slowly, adjusting to your surroundings.
- I would like you to believe that your vision is real and take it into yourself, because it is.

If you have trouble the first time you try this, do it again. Many people have never given themselves permission to quiet their minds and allow whatever comes in to have the time and space to emerge. You can take yourself away from the bustle of life into nature or another benign place for several hours, with no agenda, with technology turned off, and be with yourself to vision and to think. You can meditate, keep a journal, walk, exercise, do yoga or tai chi. The key is to *quiet* your mind and give yourself permission to *just be* and observe what your quieted mind can tell you— and wants to tell you.

Now that you have experienced your vision and internalized what it feels like for it to have already happened, it's important for you to create a *visual* reminder for yourself.

Here are two suggestions:

1. First, take a nice, long, *silent* walk to internalize what you saw and felt. Then come back and physically manifest it. Create what the Native Peoples call a mandela or what others call a shield, a crest, or anything

in any form that represents, symbolizes, or is a picture for you—a picture of your vision. Use whatever materials you wish to do this: paint, markers, paper, pictures, items of meaning, or something else. It can be three-dimensional or two-dimensional—anything at all. Then keep your creation in sight so that you are inspired and reinforced to move proactively toward your vision every day.

2. Write a story for yourself about what you saw, heard, smelled, and felt. Make the story as complete as you can and as rich as you can, with as many details as you like or just the heart of it—whatever works for you.

The last step in visioning is for you to test your vision against four qualities of a great vision. Often people think that they have a vision, but when it's put to the test, either it's a mission (purpose), it's too complicated, or it's not clear enough to understand. Rather than risk any of those potholes in your journey, simply give your vision the Great Vision Test.

Four Qualities of a Great Vision[3]

Ask yourself, "Is my vision . . . ?"

Inspiring. My vision is worth committing my time and life force to. It means something. I feel deeply passionate about it. It gives me the energy to do the day-in, day-out work. My vision inspires others when they hear me talk about it.

Clear. My vision creates a clear picture of my desired results. It serves as a useful template or set of criteria against which to create goals and evaluate my progress. When others hear my vision, they also get a clear picture of where I am going and can see how they might be able to join with me.

Credible. My vision should stretch the sense of what's possible in the present, so that it pulls me into a new and better future. It may challenge my beliefs and paradigms, so it must also ultimately be believable, for if the stretch between current reality and the imagined future is too great, it can weaken my vision's credibility and my commitment.

Commitment. I am fully committed to this vision. I did not choose this vision because it seemed like a good idea or the right thing to do. I own it. I embody it. I will do whatever is necessary to take it from a vision to a reality.

In the end, all three parts of your life, values, mission, and vision, must be aligned, or none of them will work very well for you. For instance, if your vision is to climb Mt. Everest, your mission is to teach, and your number one value is focused on building wealth, you might (or might not) have a big disconnect. If you do have a big disconnect, your life is bound to be scattered, and you are likely to be disappointed. You might find a way to connect all three, but you may have to really work at it!

I'd like to share one last thought with you about personal mastery: because we are human beings, not human *doings*, we have to make the space and time to focus on our own journey and growth. We certainly can. It is all about choices.

Key Learnings for Personal Mastery

1. Learning occurs by moving from not knowing to knowing through awareness, feedback, and then practice and experience.
2. The four competency areas of Emotional Intelligence are self-awareness, self-management, social awareness, and relationship management.
3. Extraversion and Introversion are about energy; Sensing and iNtuition are about information; Thinking and Feeling are about decisions; Judging and Perceiving are about action.
4. The Z model for decision making uses the four MBTI functions of S/N and T/F together to help make better decisions.
5. Three challenges for self-directed growth and change are:
   • Knowing whom you want to become
   • Getting feedback about how you are perceived
   • Practicing new skills and behaviors
6. Identifying your core values, your personal mission, and your future vision are all very important if you are to lead yourself and others authentically, with clarity and confidence.

PART 3

INTERPERSONAL MASTERY

Chapter 9

What Is Interpersonal Mastery?

When a leader whispers, it is often heard as a shout.
—R. B. Hewertson

It's About the Relationship; It's About the Conversation

Definition: Interpersonal mastery is having integrated the Emotional Intelligence competencies and the dialogue skills to interact successfully with other people.

Your ability to communicate and work well with others is a key foundational skill set if you want to keep and excel at your job. That's not hyperbole. It's a fact. How many people do you know or know about who are no longer in their jobs because they "could not play well with others"? It's rarely one's lack of technical skills that cause the problem. In fact, anyone who studies this topic knows that consistently, the percentage of job losses caused by lack of technical skills is rarely more than 10 to 12 percent. You don't have to study it, though. Just be observant.

The rest, are, well, the rest. Losing one's job involuntarily is usually the result of a values clash and/or poor interpersonal skills (layoffs and shutdowns aside). You may think your interpersonal skills are working well for you, and maybe they are. And—I hope you will agree—there is always room for improvement.

Communicating and working effectively with the people on your team, across teams, and throughout your organization is essential. Saying, "We need to improve communication" is a lot like saying, "We need to stop the glaciers from melting." People may want to do these things, but often they are too amorphous, too big, too everything—and we become overwhelmed and do little or nothing except throw our hands in the air or sigh in silent resignation.

We're going to make a big dent in the too big and too amorphous communication challenge right here and right now. We are going to focus on the real conversations we have with other people and improve them.

I'm sure you remember the Emotional Intelligence concepts we covered in our discussion of personal mastery. The relationship management cluster includes inspirational leadership, influence, conflict management, coach and mentor, and teamwork. None of these competencies work well without good dialogue skills. Can you recall what you listed as your EI strengths and challenges? If not, take another look in your notebook.

There will always be challenges with relationship management. Remember, people are messy! That's why interpersonal mastery and team mastery are two big parts of this book, and it's why I want to help you increase and deepen those competencies.

Seriously, all of our work gets done through people, in one way or another—one relationship at a time and one conversation at a time. When conversations work well, everything and everyone works better—and vice versa.

I'd like you to consider this: communication is about what the other person hears and understands—not what you thought you said or even intended to say.

Conversations between people, whoever they are and wherever they are, "go south" for two main reasons:

- The people involved have different and sometimes opposing expectations, values, styles, ideas, needs, or concerns.
- Something happens or is said within the communication that creates a misunderstanding and/or a conflict of some kind.

As Susan Scott says in her book *Fierce Conversations*, "When the conversation stops, the relationship stops."[1] That's just common sense, and yet we tend to ignore it much of the time, perhaps hoping that it isn't really true. Well, it *is* true. She also tells us, "Great conversations are *not* soft skills," and, "What gets talked about, how it gets talked about and who talks about it *equals* what is and what is not going to happen."[2]

Deciding to have high-quality conversations is both a choice and a *mindset*. Having good dialogue skills to create those high-quality conversations is a *skill set*. We need to want to and then truly pay close attention to our conversations and our relationships. What's in it for you? Well, the payoff is that you are far more likely to achieve great business results and enjoy your work and home life a lot more!

It starts with each of us, and it ends with each of us. That means that our personal choices about how and what we communicate have a significant impact on outcomes. Since we are all going to be in many relationships during our lifetime, it's a sure bet that we will experience and witness interpersonal conflicts and have some communication challenges. Remember, people and groups are messy!

I'd like you to think about the two questions in Exercise 13 and write your answers in your notebook.

Exercise 13

1. What are your *biggest blocks* to high-quality conversations?
2. What are your *most important* relationships at work and personally?

If you answered the first question with things like time, skills, patience, or motivation, your list is very similar to many others'. We also say that our relationships with our closest friends, significant other, direct reports, boss, children, mother, father, aunt, and so on, all matter to us. The questions we must ask are, "Are we making the time; do we have the skills; do we demonstrate the patience and does our motivation line up with our behaviors within those important relationships? Or do we take them for granted? You know that what you nurture will grow. What you don't, won't, right? It's another simple lesson from nature that we often forget.

Again, in your notebook, answer the question in Exercise 14.

Exercise 14
Solutions to Blocks

What are some *solutions* to *your* blocks to high-quality conversations?

If you mentioned revisiting your priority setting, leading more than managing, paying attention to your calendar, managing e-mail and meetings better, your attitude, learning new skills, or your choices, then you are on the right path.

The great news is, we can decide to pay attention, and we can get very skillful at communicating well and building healthy and trusting relationships. All we have to do is decide that we want to learn and then make it a priority to practice, practice, and practice some more.

There is a world of wisdom out there about communication techniques, tools, and so forth. I'm going to share with you what I *know* works for most people most of the time. When we have completed our work on interpersonal mastery, you will be far more aware of the traps that await you, you will have learned skills and have tools to avoid those traps, and be able to get yourself out of a trap if you fall into it. And you will fall in—we all do. You will be far better prepared to resolve issues quickly and with less anxiety. You will also be able to recover gracefully when you mess up.

These tools are easy to learn, use, and put into practice. I have found them to be practical and things you can apply right now to measurably benefit you in most situations. We are going to focus on three core dialogue skills:

Deep listening. This is the kind of listening for which the Dalai Lama, Oprah Winfrey, and Bill Clinton are famous. Each of them deeply listens as if the person he or she is talking with is the most important person in the world at that moment—and perhaps the person is.
Constructive feedback. This skill will draw upon deep listening as you navigate through tough or even affirming conversations in a respectful and productive way. When it is done well, constructive feedback is a tool that prevents conflicts from arising and builds trusting relationships.

Conflict management (and transformation). We'll learn simple techniques that will calm people and situations, identify root causes, and focus on solutions so that conflicts can be transformed and/or come to resolution in a neutral zone. These techniques can help build stronger relationships, better teams, and a more resilient organization.

Before we dive into these skills, let's get clear on what dialogue *is* and what it *is not.* For our purposes, dialogue is defined as a two-way process involving two actions:

Advocacy: sharing what I want, think, know, feel, and believe
Inquiry: discovering what you want, think, know, feel, and believe

Figure 9.1 shows a simple chart created by Chris Argyris that demonstrates this.[3] You can do this along with me—just take out a piece of paper and a pen, draw a box, and divide it into four equal quadrants.

Advocacy is on the vertical axis, and inquiry is on the horizontal axis. As I talk about these, consider whether you are reminded of anyone in each quadrant. Jot down the names of people you think of on the chart as we go along. I'd also like you to consider and write in what percentage of your own interactions happen within each of the four quadrants.

In the upper left quadrant, we are high on advocacy and low on inquiry. This means that we are only sharing our story, so we are primarily *telling*—not making space to listen.

Figure 9.1   Dialogue

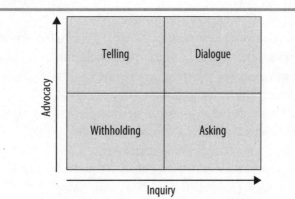

In the lower left quadrant, we have low advocacy, so we are not sharing our story, but we also have low inquiry, meaning that we are not asking about another person's story either—this looks and feels like *withholding*.

In the lower right quadrant, we are high on inquiry and low on advocacy. That means we are *asking* another person a lot of questions without sharing any of our own story. If we do this too much, it feels a lot like an interrogation.

Finally, in the upper right quadrant, we are at a high level of both advocacy and inquiry. This encourages two-way conversation. This is where *real dialogue* takes place. Being high on both advocacy and inquiry means that we are fully engaged with the other person. We are balanced between sharing our story and discovering the other person's story.

Each quadrant can work perfectly well at the right time and the right place. For instance, if a woman in front of you drops her wallet, you need to be telling her about that, and really not much else. And if your dog is missing, you need to be out there asking the question, "Have you seen my lost dog?" This isn't likely to be a time when you want or need to hear about your neighbor having lost his dog 10 years ago. You get my point.

For our purposes, we will focus on relationship-building dialogue skills and improving them in a balanced way. We want our work and personal conversations to move us forward, not backward. In the dialogue quadrant, advocacy and inquiry are happening at a deeper level than simply asking or telling. Here are some examples:

1. Advocacy: statement-oriented first
   - State your view.
   - State your assumptions and/or data.
   - Share what you are thinking and what led you to that view.
   - Give examples that led you to your conclusions.
   - Encourage others to explore your view.
2. Inquiry: question-oriented first
   - Understand the other person's view before advocating yours.
   - Listen without resistance.
   - Draw out the other person's reasoning.
   - Explain your reasons for inquiring.
   - Test by asking for broader contexts and examples.

3. Keys to authentic dialogue
   - Attitude: do you want to learn or do you want to control?
   - Utilize inquiry and advocacy in a balanced way.
   - Pay attention to what you and others are doing, saying, and not saying.
   - Notice whether one or both people are engaged in the conversation.
   - Pay attention to the degree of genuine interest for mutual understanding versus one or the other wanting to control or be "right."

Dialogue skills, when utilized well, increase mutual understanding, can prevent little problems from becoming big problems, and add a noticeable richness to relationships. Interpersonal mastery is not possible without good dialogue skills. There is no silver bullet; becoming skilled requires mindfulness, motivation, and mastery. And that means we need to practice. So let's get started!

Chapter 10

DEEP LISTENING

If you are not listening . . . you are not leading.
—R. B. HEWERTSON

Most people do not listen with the intent to understand;
they listen with the intent to reply.
—STEPHEN R. COVEY

I cannot recall where I heard this, but it really stuck with me: "Listening well is a lot like justice. It must be done . . . and . . . it must be believed to have been done." Deep listening is the most important of the dialogue skills because it supports all the others. Without deep listening, constructive feedback and conflict transformation cannot happen well, if they happen at all.

The ability to listen deeply and well is:

- A learned skill that can become a great habit with practice and attention.
- The number one skill to prevent and defuse conflict.
- The primary skill for increasing engagement and motivation.
- The primary skill for increasing trust with your staff, boss, coworkers, and family.

There is no downside to becoming a habitually great listener. You will be heard precisely because you listen well. Listening well is the one habit that you won't ever want to break.

In our culture, we spend a lot of time being talked *at*—in school, at home, and at work. We have become experts in talking *at* people. Conversely, most of us were not taught how to listen deeply to others. And yet this skill is highly valued in everyone, especially leaders. I am serious when I say, "If you are not listening, you are not leading." It is that simple. When leaders don't listen well, other strengths they may have will be greatly diminished or even canceled out.

People pay more attention to what we do than to what we say. This is particularly true for leaders. Make no mistake about it: this has a big impact on your credibility and on how much people will trust you, so it's a good idea to make sure that what you are *saying* and what you are *doing* actually line up.

I expect you know that we listen with more than our ears—we also use our eyes, our instincts, and our heart to take in and interpret what someone is doing and saying or not saying. People who are deaf have a very keen awareness of their other four senses in order to compensate, and they can "listen" very well without any sound.

Messages can come from words, tone, body movements, cadence, rhythm, and even the almost invisible clues associated with the 43 muscles in our face. Together, these are all pieces of the communication puzzle. They tell us much more of the story than words alone can convey. This is another great reason not to rely on e-mail for communication!

Researchers may argue about the exact percentages, but there is wide agreement that the vast majority of human communication is nonverbal, with some researchers even putting it as high as 93 percent! You may or may not be aware that there are, at a minimum, seven universal human emotions: happiness, contempt, sadness, surprise, fear, anger, and disgust. Yet, even without knowing this, most people, the world over, are able to read these seven emotions on other people's faces, no matter how hard someone is trying to hide them. So indeed, we listen with our eyes, our ears, our instincts, and our hearts.

The bigger question is: Are we paying attention? Deep listening requires us to focus on the person in front of us and truly take in all of what he is saying. So, what gets in the way of our paying attention?

Rob is the founding CEO of a very successful company. He is charismatic, passionate, a visionary, smart, funny, energetic, and . . . loud. He knows that he has listening challenges, but still, in a meeting with several members of a project team, he took up most of the "airtime" with his ideas. As people were leaving the room, Rob mentally slapped himself and quickly asked them to come back in. He said, "You know, I really never gave any of you enough time or space to tell me what you really think, and I absolutely want to know what you really think." The team came back in, and an hour later, Rob had deeply listened and was able to stay quiet long enough to hear a brilliant idea that would end up saving his company several million dollars.

Rob is an energetic overtalker. The rest of us may find that we have one or more of our own bad listening habits. We are not truly listening or paying attention to the speaker when we are doing a lot of other things like:

- Judging
- Talking or arguing
- Editing
- Planning how to "fix" the situation
- Rehearsing a response
- Working on e-mail, phone, or computer
- Thinking of advice to give; "fixing"
- Interrupting
- Thinking of something or someone else
- Making the conversation about you
- "One-upping" the speaker
- Focusing on one person in a group

I'm sure you can think of more bad habits. In fact, I'd like you to think about three common situations and take the time to answer the questions in Exercise 15 about each one for yourself.

Exercise 15
Think of a Time When . . .

1. You experienced people talking over one another. Who was there, and how did it make you feel? Did you notice what you did when this happened? How did others respond?

(Continued)

2. Someone you knew was *not listening to you*, and you knew it. Who was it, and what did this person do or say to make you believe that they were not really listening? How did you feel during and after that interaction?
3. You were talking with someone and you *knew this person was totally focused on you* and was hearing everything that you said and meant. Who was it? What did this person do or say to make you believe that they were really listening to you? How did you feel during and after that interaction?

It's pretty clear, isn't it? We know when we are being heard, respected, and valued. If it's true for you, you can bet that it's true for everyone you interact with at work and in your personal life. In my life, I have nearly lost important relationships because I was talking *at* people I love, filling in spaces with my words, and not listening deeply to what they wanted and needed to say. I tend to be a problem solver. Instead of being empathic, I can quickly jump into being a "fix-it" person. Fortunately, over the years, my family, friends, and colleagues have done a good job of raising my awareness. I practice deep listening skills, and I succeed in using them much more of the time; and still, just like you, I need to keep working at it.

I expect you have learned most, if not all, of the following information about listening in the past. Still, perhaps some clarity of perspective and timely reminders will be helpful to you.

Deep listening requires being mindful of two big things—our *focus* and *attitude* toward the person who is speaking.

The behaviors that demonstrate a deep listening *focus* are:

- Paraphrase or restate what the person has just said. This indicates that you are listening carefully and that you understand both the details and the meaning of what was said.
- Summarize the major ideas or themes of what was said.
- Give nonverbal indications of attentiveness, including maintaining eye contact (without staring), sitting up, nodding, paying attention, and perhaps leaning forward, so that your body is telegraphing that you are interested, not bored.
- Use verbal indications of attentiveness, such as, "Yes, I see," "Uh-huh," "Mmmm," "Aha," or "Really?"

The behaviors that demonstrate a deep listening *attitude* are:

- *Convey empathy.* "I understand; it sounds like you feel . . ." This includes an attitude of positive acceptance and demonstrates that you accept and value the person and her feelings. You don't have to agree with what she is saying, but you are still showing interest and attempting to understand her point of view.
- *Encourage the conversation* by asking the person to, "Tell me more about . . ." or "Please help me understand more about . . ." Verbally indicate that you are paying attention, you are interested, and you want to hear more from him. "I see what you mean; tell me more about why that is difficult for you."
- *Use positive body language* by keeping yourself open and accepting, and do nothing that is threatening or disrespectful.

For even deeper listening—when you want to fully understand the story behind the story or the question behind the question—you need to master the skill of drawing the person deeper into the conversation and digging for "gold" without interrogating.

There are at least three ways to do this:

- *Mining.* This is exploring more about the emotions involved and getting at the real issues. Ask how a person is feeling and why. "And how does that make you feel? How did this whole thing begin? So what is the meaning of this for you?" Then really listen to the answers.
- *Clarifying.* Ask the person to clarify various points to help you connect the dots, so that you can truly understand what is important to her. "Could you tell me more about . . . ?" "Is this what you meant?" "Does that mean . . . ?" Then really listen to her answers.
- *Expanding.* This is building on paraphrasing by helping the person developing his ideas fully, taking something that you think he is saying or that you perceive he is conveying and saying what he hasn't said yet. "So are you saying that . . . ?" or, "Given that this is happening, are you feeling . . . ?" Then really listen to his answers.

Often people will not share because they are not sure whether or not you want to hear their story, or because they are embarrassed, or just because they are not used to having someone truly listen to them. You will often hear important information if you gently ask a few questions to draw out the person and then allow silence to fill the air space until the other person chooses to speak. This will also help the person feel and believe that you are genuinely interested.

I think you will agree that in our culture in general, we need to take more turns listening instead of taking more turns talking. In the American culture, we tend to reward extraversion and thinking out loud, forgetting that at least half of the wisdom or thoughts in any conversation are within the other person, who may or may not "talk to think." In our meetings and in our personal lives, we need to make sure that the "tyranny of the loud" does not rule, and remember that the person who speaks first or loudest is not automatically qualified to lead the conversation! In conversations, extraverts need to take a breath and consciously make space for and invite others to speak, and introverts need to step into the space to be sure that their voices are heard.

Let's see how you think you are doing with the skill of deep listening. Using your notebook, write down next to each numbered question in Exercise 16 a score of 1 to 5, with 5 being high, to indicate how well you believe you do these 10 things. Then answer the four questions that follow to explore a bit more.

Exercise 16
Deep Listening Checklist

Score yourself on a scale of 1 to 5, with 5 being high.

1. Paraphrasing _____
2. Summarizing _____
3. Giving nonverbal attentiveness _____
4. Giving verbal attentiveness _____
5. Conveying empathy _____
6. Encouraging the conversation _____
7. Positive body language _____
8. Mining _____
9. Clarifying _____
10. Expanding _____

- What are your listening strengths?
- Where could you do better with listening?
- What might people at work say about your listening skills?
- What might people in your personal life say about your listening skills?

Three absolute *Do Nots* when you are supposed to be listening are:

1. *Do not* use judgmental words or tones; do not say that something or someone is stupid, ridiculous, or bad; do not evaluate.
2. *Do not* attempt to solve or "fix" the problem unless someone explicitly asks for your help in fixing something. Before you jump in, stop and think—is it wise for you to be doing the fixing?
3. *Do not* suggest that someone's feelings are wrong or right; they just are what they are. Feelings come from values and are the source of how people behave. Understanding someone's feelings is a key to understanding the person.
   Few of us will become perfect at deep listening—that's not the point. The point is to be mindful, pay attention, and become as skilled as you can. It requires awareness, first. Becoming skilled also requires a sincere motivation on your part to make the time and take the effort to deeply listen to the people in your life. Everyone you deeply listen to will feel heard, respected, and valued. Those powerful feelings build trust and loyalty. The reverse, of course, is also true.

Chapter 11

CONSTRUCTIVE FEEDBACK

That which we persist in doing becomes easier—not that the nature of the task has changed, but our ability to do has increased.
—RALPH WALDO EMERSON

Let's say your listening skills are serving you well, and still, those inevitable tough conversations are a concern. Before we get immersed in constructive feedback, I would like you to take out your notebook and answer the three questions in Exercise 17 without thinking too hard; just respond from your gut.

Exercise 17

1. What are all the thoughts, words, and emotions that you have when you hear the word *feedback*?
2. Think about someone with whom you want or need to share some challenging or perhaps difficult information regarding his or her behavior or actions. Who is that person?
3. Why haven't you done it?

When I ask leaders the first question, there are a number of common responses:

"Oh, no; here it comes," "Criticism," "What did I do now?," "Learning," "It's information I need, so give it to me straight," "Really, now?," "Get ready," "Defensive," "Bad news," "Painful," "Useful." The reactions are always mixed, but the vast majority of them are stress-inducing and negative.

People respond this way because both the term and the action of feedback have been misused, abused, and often delivered poorly in most people's life experience.

In the second question, you'll notice that I didn't limit whom you could choose or what the information was about. It could be a little thing or a big thing, at home or at work. Consider why you chose the person you chose.

For the third question, here are some frequent responses, and you may have others: "I don't want to rock the boat," "I don't know how to start," "I'm afraid of what will happen," "I've tried it before and nothing changed," "If I ignore it long enough, it will fix itself," "I don't want to hurt anyone," "I'm afraid of what he will say or do," "Maybe it's my fault," "It's probably not that important," and "It's not my job to tell her."

Did any of those reasons sound familiar to you? I expect at least one of them did.

Is it any wonder that we do such a lousy job at giving constructive feedback? There is a good deal of fear that keeps us from dealing with uncomfortable subjects. I know of cases where people are losing sleep and becoming anxious, worried, and fretful just because they need to have an important conversation, but they don't know how to start it or they are having trouble getting past their fears. It is affecting their lives in more ways than one. Not good.

We have a boatload of experience with these conversations and reasons for why we're not starting one. Most of us would prefer to avoid pain rather than invite it. The irony is that most of the time, giving constructive feedback well will actually *prevent* much more pain down the road.

What if you could have a tool in your interpersonal mastery toolbox that would help you do this well? Wouldn't that relieve some of your concern? Let's explore how to reframe this whole dialogue skill in your mind. First, let's understand what constructive feedback really is:

Definition: Constructive Feedback is information about the impact of a behavior or action.

The information itself is not negative or positive; it's just information. The behaviors that you are giving the information about may be positive or negative, but information is truly neutral. Furthermore, information is a *gift* to the receiver because without it, he is unaware and operating in the dark.

Not only is constructive feedback a gift, but it is also the kindest thing you can do for someone who is getting in her own way. To leave her hanging out there is cruel. It's the "emperor with no clothes" syndrome, and who wants to be a fool?

Consider this: Would you want to have spinach on your teeth before a big presentation, or would you hope that someone would care enough to tell you? I know I want to be told of anything I'm doing or saying that is getting in the way of my being the best I can be, and I expect you do as well.

Furthermore, we spend too little time giving constructive feedback about positive actions and behaviors. This is more than a "thank you." It's being specific about what the person did and why it mattered, and encouraging him to continue this action or behavior. Ken Blanchard and Spencer Johnson, in their classic book *The One Minute Manager*, said it best: "Catch people doing things right."[1] This sage advice has not gone out of style and never will, but today, more than 30 years later, it *still* hasn't become common practice. We know from all the research and from our own experience that people respond far better to being and feeling *appreciated* by those who matter to them than to just about anything else.

As leaders, we must model giving *and* receiving constructive feedback. Giving it well matters because it is critically important for healthy business relationships and cultures. Inviting feedback about yourself is important because, as a leader, you have little knowledge about your impact on people without it. It's better to ask about your impact and know what it is before it's too late.

There are few leaders who do a great job of either giving or asking for feedback. I am not guessing or judging; this is a fact. The aggregate 360-degree feedback data on the literally thousands of leaders and staff I have had in my courses show ratings somewhat to significantly below the middle for the statement, "This leader/individual asks for constructive feedback." The rating for giving constructive feedback is slightly higher, but it's still not great.

Constructive feedback is a valuable tool, but just like any other tool, it can be used to *build* or to *destroy*. It is the responsibility of the giver to provide the information in such a way that the receiver can hear it, and to use the tool properly. It's the responsibility of the receiver to listen carefully, take in the information, and then make choices about what to do with it.

In every single organization, management team, and family, there are "group secrets." These are the things that everyone knows, but no one talks about to the person or people who are involved. You know what I mean. It's Bill, who is flirting with the new woman in Department D, and it's Pat, who isn't carrying her weight on the project, but she's close to retirement so people are saying that's why she gets away with it. Every group and every family has its "secrets" that aren't really secret at all.

These things may start out in the minor leagues, but they often don't stay that way. Sooner or later, the stinky little "poop piles" (my term!) become big toxic waste dumps. They can lead to serious conflicts, and they rarely go away on their own.

It's a very good idea for you to clean up your smaller sticky and stinky messes before they become toxic waste. Yes, it takes time and sometimes courage, but it takes *far* less time than it will if and when things blow up. I'm about to give you a new tool.

It's constructive feedback, and it is your *super-duper pooper-scooper!*

Before I share a method that I know works well and that you can begin applying immediately, I'd like to debunk several old schools of thought about how to give feedback. It amazes me that some of these methods are still taught and used. They are simply awful, and all of them contribute to feedback having a bad name.

The mud sandwich. This is the method where we tell someone how wonderful she is, then tell her how and why she stinks, and then tell her how wonderful she is again. People are "waiting for the shoe to drop," and their defensive walls will pop up immediately. We can get away with this only once before people are on to us. Do not use the happy, crappy, happy method of feedback. It's a setup, and people hate it. Oh, and by the way, it doesn't work.

The yes but. This is a close cousin to the mud sandwich. When the words that come out of your mouth are, "Yes, that was fine, but," the *but* is all that people hear. Anything that was said before the *but* is disregarded, even though we think we are being ever so nice, giving great feedback, and just making it clear what could be better. In the end, people begin to feel that they can *never* live up to your expectations, so they will eventually stop trying. Get rid of the *but*!

. *The dance.* With this method, we never really say what we need to say. Instead, we dance around the topic and totally confuse the person. The irony is that we may think we gave him feedback, but we probably didn't because he probably couldn't decipher it. It is really the coward's way out to kinda, sorta, maybe, almost tell someone what you need to tell him.

The drive-by. In this case, wherever and whenever we decide that something we want to say works for us, we hit her between the eyes as we wander by. We just tell the person that we think she stinks and may even tell her why, and then we walk away. Some people believe that this is the best way to give feedback because it's quick and clean; it's done, dusted, and no fluff—just the facts, and telling them straight. The problem is, this technique *isn't clean.*

The interpersonal mess, resentment, and/or anger that it creates are predictable and problematic—and that means that it *isn't quick or effective* either.

The Six Steps for Constructive Feedback tool that I am about to give you will improve your communication and your relationships—a lot.

Six Steps for Constructive Feedback

1. Prepare.
   - Consider the time and place—where and when is this conversation taking place, and why?
   - Consider emotional issues, yours and his.
   - Consider the person and his style—how should you convey this information so that he can hear it?
   - Know *why* (your motivation) you are giving this constructive feedback.
   - Mentally prepare, and make notes as needed.
2. Convey positive intent (advocacy).
   - Share your reason for wanting this conversation (your motivation).
   - Point to a common goal.
   - Your motivation must be for improvement or development, not blame.
   - Briefly state what you would like to discuss and why, using *I* statements.

3. Describe what you have observed (advocacy).
   - Be specific, concise, and to the point—give clear example(s) of the person's behaviors and/or actions.
   - Focus on the behaviors or actions, not on the person or his qualities.
4. State the impact of the behaviors or actions (advocacy).
   - Link the behaviors or actions to the impact on yourself, the business, or others.
   - State one or two consequences that you believe will result if nothing changes.
5. Ask the other person to respond (inquiry).
   - Ask open-ended questions.
   - Listen without becoming defensive.
   - Keep the focus on the topic and the other person, and be open to receiving feedback if it is relevant.
   - Summarize.
6. Focus the discussion on solutions, not blame (dialogue).
   - Model inquiry and advocacy.
   - When appropriate, ask for the change you hope for.
   - Be willing to help support the change if that would be helpful.
   - Be open, ask for, and listen to solution ideas—brainstorm.
   - Mutually select solutions.
   - Identify the next steps, follow-up, and a timeline.

I am going to assume that you really understand why it's important to prepare. Using this tool off the top of your head, ad hoc, willy-nilly, is neither smart nor likely to succeed. Preparation gives you a huge leg up in doing it well.

Let's talk about Step 2, "convey positive intent," a bit more. This is *the* step that most people either forget or somehow turn into a mud sandwich or "yes, but," and it's *the most important step* to get right. Think of it this way: it is in *your best interest* as well as the other person's to keep his defensive walls from popping up. Agreed? OK, then the way you do that is to be really clear about why you want to share information with him about something that matters to both of you. When you get this right, the rest will flow.

Let's say your peer, Pete, has a habit of showing up exactly 10 minutes late for every biweekly project meeting, and you find yourself and others looking at your watches and getting snippy with him even outside the meeting. It's definitely time for constructive feedback.

Conveying your *positive intent* might look like this:

(Private conversation.) "Pete, I value our partnership, and I would like it to stay on solid ground. There's something I would like to share with you that could put our partnership at risk. Is now a good time, or can we set something up for another time this week?"

Pete might say, "Sure, now's great. What's up, and what do you mean at risk?" Go to Step 3 and describe what you have observed.

"Pete, in our biweekly project meetings, I have noticed, as has everyone in that group, that you are predictably 10 minutes late. This causes all of us to either scramble to catch you up or waste time waiting for you when we need your input."

Pete says, "Gee, I thought that only happened once or twice. Are you sure?"

You say, "Yes, Pete, it's happened in five of the last six meetings."

Go to Step 4. "I'm concerned about both the impact on the meeting and the impact on how people feel about your participation. I know we're all busy and short on time, so when you're late, it sends the group a message that you think your time is more important than theirs. I doubt that you want to send that message, am I right?"

Pete nods, and you go to Step 5. "So what are you thinking, Pete?"

Pete says, "Sorry, I really didn't think it was that big a deal. Every week before your meeting, I have a full-staff meeting that usually ends at the same time that yours starts, and it's all the way on the other side of the complex. I get here as fast as I can, but it takes me at least 10 minutes to get here."

Step 6 is all about focusing on solutions. "Gee, I had no idea you were back to back. Let's brainstorm what you can do and/or what I can do to make this more workable and still have our meeting start on time. I'd like to get this solved for both of us before our next session. Any ideas?"

Pete says, "Maybe we could start our meeting at a different time, or maybe we can let everyone know about the situation and make sure that no agenda items involving me are scheduled for the first 10 minutes."

You and Pete are now well on your way to a solution.

Notice that in this example, I never used the word *feedback*. You don't need it, and frankly, I'd ditch it in conversation because it has been so maligned. A situation that could have degenerated into sarcasm, a smudge on someone's reputation, a growing lack of trust, resentment, or some other problem was solved because of *the conversation*.

Not all situations are that easy, of course. Still, many of them are. We get into a lot of trouble and make stupid mistakes when we make assumptions about other people's motivations and potential reactions. Pete is a great example—he wasn't being disrespectful on purpose; he had a simple logistical problem, and he was totally unaware that other people cared about his presence as much as they did. It is easy to see how everyone got sideways on this one, isn't it?

This may feel awkward to you at first. In fact, I am fairly sure it will. Going through these steps in *exactly* this order is important, and putting each step into your own words to fit the person and the situation is just as important. It often helps to circle back to your positive intent and to stay focused on the issue while staying open to hearing the other person's perception of reality.

We all bring our authority issues to work with us. When you are the boss, people know that you are the boss and behave differently with you because of this. Really they do. Keep this in mind as you are preparing your feedback; it may help you focus on your positive intent and help the other person hear the meaning of what you are saying. Remember, it's not constructive if it is something else—anything else.

CONSTRUCTIVE FEEDBACK CHALLENGES

Any skill set has its challenges. Here are some to be on the lookout for when you are giving and receiving constructive feedback.

When *giving* feedback, you may find it *hard* to:
- Remember that constructive feedback is the *kindest* and *most respectful* thing you can do when you carry it out with respect.
- Leave room for problem solving rather than telling the person what to do.
- State your feedback in a way that conveys respect and support.
- Get to the point.
- Respond to what the person receiving feedback says without defensiveness.
- Give feedback to someone whom you don't know well, over whom you have no authority, or who has authority over you.

- Provide clear examples that relate directly to your concern.
- Not pull other parties' opinions and experiences into the conversation without their permission.

When *receiving* feedback, you may find it *hard* to:

- Listen objectively without interrupting.
- Avoid taking feedback so personally that you become defensive.
- Avoid justifying your behaviors or actions.
- Respond constructively if you feel that you are under attack.
- Always say thank you for the person's courage, honesty, and taking the time, even if you don't like or agree with the information.
- Hear the truth within the feedback and take appropriate action.
- Welcome suggestions.
- Be humble.
- Be solution-oriented.

Highly effective leaders make a point of asking for and appreciate honest feedback from their peers and their direct reports as well as from customers and their own leader. When this skill is part of the workplace culture, it opens up lines of communication, reduces fear, and supports a healthy workplace.

In order to believe that you have "conscious competence" with constructive feedback, you need to practice it. Take out your notebook and work through the process as noted in Exercise 18.

Exercise 18
Practicing Constructive Feedback

1. Choose your own situation (for example, someone to whom you need to give constructive feedback, but you have not done so) to help you practice the six steps.
2. Prepare your conversation. Decide when and where you will have this conversation and, generally, what you will say in your own words, using the next five steps in exactly that order.
3. *Practice* the conversation with someone you trust or out loud, if that will help.
4. Evaluate your approach.
5. Do it again and again until you feel prepared. Then choose another person and situation and practice some more.

Constructive Feedback Practice

Once you become comfortable with your approach to constructive feedback, it will become a natural part of how you communicate. To integrate *any* new behavior, you need to make it a priority and incorporate it into your daily life. There are four kinds of feedback situations that I suggest you practice regularly.

Four Constructive Feedback Practices to Build into Your Daily Life

Practice 1

Encourage someone. Use your constructive feedback skills to share with this person specifically what she is doing well and/or what you appreciate. Do this as often as possible with as many people as you can to help integrate the skill yourself. It will feel good to you and will be appreciated by the other person.

Practice 2

Prepare and practice a potentially tough conversation, as you did in Exercise 18. Consider how you will convey your positive intention authentically. Remember to check your motivation. Don't get stuck thinking about what the person might say or do. Do what you believe will have the highest chance of being heard by that person.

Practice 3

Ask for feedback on your own behaviors and actions. Review your current responsibilities (you can do this with your family responsibilities as well as your work responsibilities). Identify your top two responsibilities. Ask people you trust to be candid with you about your performance in the two areas that really matter to you and are important to your success. Listen carefully, without interrupting, defensiveness, or justifying yourself. Enlist a few people you trust to give you regular input. When you ask for constructive feedback and respond well, most people will be more than happy to keep helping you.

Practice 4

If you have a team, your team members should ask for performance feedback from the team's stakeholders from time to time. This will help them be better informed, learn to be open rather than defensive, and be more effective. Asking for feedback comes with a warning: ask only when you and your team are ready to hear and act upon the answers you receive.

Once you have become more comfortable with giving and receiving feedback, you will find it to be highly effective in preventing conflicts and correcting problems before they get out of hand. This skill also helps you build strong and trusting relationships. When constructive feedback becomes a normal and healthy habit for you, new lines of communication will open up for you and fear of truth telling will diminish greatly.

Make time to practice often, and soon you will be able to recognize those moments when you know that something needs to be said and you will be confident in doing something about it.

Chapter 12

MANAGING "UP"

No one can make you feel inferior without your consent.
—ELEANOR ROOSEVELT

What is managing "up"? Here's a way to think about it:

Definition: Managing up is the act of consciously building successful relationships with your leader and those in positions of greater authority, to enhance your success and that of your leader and organization.

In the previous chapter, we talked about constructive feedback and the importance of having those necessary conversations no matter who the person is. That's easy to say and harder to do when it's your own leader or another person in a position of authority who is having an impact on you and your work. I'm going to help you have those tough conversations.

Take out your notebook now and answer the questions in Exercise 19. It can be useful to have a conversation with someone you trust as you explore these questions.

Exercise 19
Managing Up

1. What are your *blocks* to managing up?
2. Why do you need to manage up in your role right now?
3. What are three ways in which you can *rethink* managing up to remove your blocks?

Create a plan of action to do those three things.

What?
When?
How?
Who?
Where?

Nearly everyone I know has, at one time or another, struggled with managing up and sharing what he knows, feels, or has to say—with his own leader. We have this fear or hesitation because we've learned it. We've learned it from our parents: "Speak when you are spoken to"; "Respect your elders." We've learned it from our schools: "Your job is to listen and learn, not to question your teacher." The message was clear and strong. Of course, it's *wrong*, but we've internalized it. However, now that we are adults and paying attention, we can choose our responses more wisely.

Have you noticed how even subtle and common word choices can influence behaviors? Consider, "She is your *superior*" and "You are his *subordinate*." It's good for us to pay attention to what our words actually mean and how we describe and/or define ourselves in relation to others. We know that *superior* means "better than" and *sub* means "under or less than." When we unconsciously adopt this language, it perpetuates a deeply internalized class system at work, rather than describing one's adult role in relation to another person's adult role. Far better words are *manager* or *leader* and *direct report*, *staff member*, or *team member*.

Of course roles and lines of authority should be acknowledged and respected. And, I believe it is far more important that we first respect human dignity, regardless of someone's "power" relationship to us.

As a new manager, I was invited to attend a three-day orientation series where all the senior administrators spoke about their areas of expertise and gave their perspective on the university's mission. On the first day, Joan, a vice provost (the only senior woman administrator at the time), gave a talk that struck a deep chord with me. She said, *"Never let anyone intimidate you, here or anywhere else in life. You have as much right to your opinion as anyone and as much ability to think good thoughts as anyone, and no one has the right to intimidate you in any way."* That concept resonated with me in a powerful way that would soon be put to the test.

In later sessions, I heard three conflicting points of view on the primary reason for the university's existence. At a break, I asked, Jack, the Controller, which was the right one. He wagged his finger just short of my nose, and said, "Listen here, you don't know anything yet, so don't ask stupid questions."

Well, I'm not all that keen on having fingers in my face, and Joan's words had hit a chord. So I put my hand up between his finger and my nose and calmly said, "Hang on, Jack; did you know that the people giving these sessions are sending three different messages to us newbies, and it's really confusing?" I gave him the facts, to which he replied, "Really? Oh, gee, I didn't realize that. Thanks for telling me." And he wandered off. That was my first interaction with Jack, but it was far from my last. From then on, he treated me with patience and respect, and I'm quite certain it was because I stood up for myself the first time he talked with me.

Fear of failure is another reason that managing up makes us nervous. What if you want to tell your leader that her curtness is alienating people, but you're afraid that she'll see you as a problem and therefore you might "fail"? Consider this compelling, if subconscious rationale: for some people, the fear of giving the leader constructive feedback is equivalent to dying—which is, of course, failing to live.

Let me prove it to you. The less-than-a-second internal dialogue goes like this: "If I give my leader feedback, he might not like it, and he might fire me; if I'm fired, I won't have any money; if I don't have any money, I can't buy food; if I don't have any food, I'll die."

Snap! Just like that, we've equated the risk of telling our truth to the leader with dying. Wow! How did that happen? It happened because the amygdala in our brain sends us all kinds of fear signals, rational or not. Unless we stop, pay attention, and put other parts of our brain to work, we'll keep letting fear rule too much in our lives.

We *all* have our authority issues. We respond to authority in our own ways, but make no mistake: we do have authority issues, and we do respond to them—and so do our people.

Then why take the risk of managing up? As much as you, as a leader, don't want to be kept in the dark, neither do other leaders. And if it is hard for you to ask for feedback, it may also be hard for your leader. Everyone needs to know when she is doing things right and when she is messing up, so giving is truly as important as receiving.

Focusing on your relationship with your leader and other decision makers within your organization's hierarchy makes sense for several reasons. Michael Feiner wrote about managing or leading up in his book *The Feiner Points of Leadership*,[1] and Michael Useem wrote more about the subject in his book *Leading Up*.[2] Here are 10 suggestions combining the wisdom from both of these wonderful authors.

1. *Take responsibility.* You are solely responsible for your half of the relationship with your leader, and you have the power to influence it.
2. *Know your leader and yourself.* You need to know your leader's style, motivation, and priorities. You need to know the same things about yourself so that you can adapt your communication style to meet his needs while meeting yours.
3. *Help your leader succeed.* No matter how engaged your leader is with you, commit yourself to your leader's success and do your job well.
4. *Keep your leader informed.* Leaders want to know what is going on and don't like surprises.
5. *Develop a network of influence.* Avoid becoming overly dependent on your leader. Build relationships with a number of leaders so that you can draw on their influence and skills when needed.
6. *Serve the mission.* If your leader rejects or ignores your appeals, or if she offers you little guidance, make your decisions based on the organization's mission and on your own core values.
7. *Build a career contract.* You have a right to receive certain things from your leader, including feedback, coaching, career counseling, and information on how things work. Ask questions and share your needs for your own development.

8. *Learn to push back.* To preserve your self-esteem and integrity, you must learn to push back and even say no, regardless of how difficult it may be. Private criticism coupled with public support will help your voice be heard. Use good dialogue skills.

9. *Maintain respect.* Never treat your leader like a fool, even if he is one. And never, ever upstage your leader. It will at least diminish you and could put you out of a job.

10. *Act grown up.* If you are not getting what you want and need, ask for it. High-performing, successful professionals don't act like or become victims; they take responsibility for their own careers and their happiness.

To help you reframe and get in the groove, answer the five questions in Exercise 20.

Exercise 20
Five Managing-Up Questions

1. What *exactly* are your expectations of your leader?
2. Are your expectations realistic and fair?
3. Have you shared these expectations with your leader?
4. What baggage with authority issues are you bringing to the table?
5. If you are already a leader, what do you want people to do and say to manage up to *you*, and have you had these important conversations?

Our constructive feedback tool is a huge help for managing up and making it a heck of a lot safer. Being objective and providing good data are important as well, no matter what the topic may be.

In the first step of constructive feedback, you prepare. This is the time to keep your leader's style, personality, and preferences in mind. Consider your own motivation and articulate your positive intent. Don't dance; be clear about your needs and your desire to help your leader in every way you can. Remember, *how* you say what you need to say is at least as important as the message you want to deliver.

What's in it for you? You and I both know that your job satisfaction and success depend on your learning to manage up well. Helping your leader succeed often helps you succeed. Neither you nor most leaders mess up on purpose. We are all human, and we are adults. You were hired because someone believed you could do the job, and therefore what you think, feel, and say should matter. Managing up is essentially no different from any other conversation or any other constructive feedback challenge. So what are *you* going to do about it?

Joan, the vice provost, said another thing that day. She said, "Don't let power, title, gender, race, age, connections, money, or anything else keep you from becoming the person you wish to become and doing what you wish to do." I took her advice to heart, and it has served me very well my entire career.

Chapter 13

Conflict Resolution and Transformation

He who angers you, conquers you.
—Elizabeth Kenny

We're going to look at conflict head on—what it is, why it happens, and how to manage and even transform conflict when it happens. Let's take a look at what happens when you experience a conflict.

Do you hold your conflict tension in your chest, fists, temples, stomach, neck, or somewhere else? Do your ears pound; does your heart thump? What actually happens that creates this physical reaction in you? For many people, anger and fear are the most likely culprits. Our bodies generally tell us what's going on before our minds can sort it out. This has been true since the beginning of human existence. It's a survival instinct that clicks in, whether the threat is real or perceived. Our brains don't know the difference immediately. When we *perceive* that we are in danger, we react. We fight, take flight, or we freeze.

As with constructive feedback, learning this dialogue skill may challenge you to make a paradigm shift. By the end of this chapter, I would like you to believe that *conflict can be healthy* and is even necessary for growth.

Many people would be delighted to never have another conflict with anyone ever again. Alas, believing or even hoping that we can avoid conflict is an illusion. Conflict will not go away. Many conflicts will fester and get worse unless they get the attention they demand. Indeed, as Carl Jung once said, "What we resist, persists." This is true whether the conflict is inside of one's self or with someone else.

Conflict is a symptom, not a disease. Conflict is a red flag that shows us where we may need to make changes, like the body having a stress headache. It can start with a misunderstanding or a hurt that turns into anger or even war. Unresolved conflict robs people and their organizations of life-giving energy that could be used for positive change, innovation, and growth. Resolved conflicts can truly make us stronger as individuals, teams, families, and organizations. Let's define conflict in, perhaps, a different way from the way you may currently think of it.

Definition: Conflict is a normal part of human interaction that arises when two or more people have opposing needs, wants, and/or expectations—real or perceived.

Does that make sense? If so, let's look at the outcomes of our own decisions around conflict and human energy.

Dysfunctional outcomes of *unresolved conflict* result in *wasted energy* that shows up in our behaviors and attitudes such as:

- Being stuck in the past
- Just getting by
- Being overly cautious
- Letting fear rule
- Staying uncomfortable
- Hiding mistakes
- Repeating old patterns
- Turf wars
- A win-lose culture

Not a pretty picture. Unfortunately, I see far too many of these outcomes in my work. Effective leaders can change this so that we get the best from people and so that we don't let all that energy leak out of our organizations.

On the other side of the coin, functional outcomes of *resolved conflict* result in *focused energy* that shows up in our behaviors and attitudes as:

- Exploring new ideas
- Sharing and learning from mistakes
- Striving together
- Willing to take reasonable risks
- Being accountable
- Being supportive
- Being courageous
- Living the values and principles
- A win-win culture

This is what we need to see in our teams, our businesses, our government, our communities, and our families. That means that we, as leaders, will need to reframe, redefine, and respond very differently to conflict situations before and when they arise—and they will.

It is a fact that no team, no matter how big, small, smart, efficient, talented, or caring it may be, will succeed for long if it has not experienced internal conflicts and resolved them effectively. When I am helping leaders build their teams, I make a point of identifying a conflict that the team must resolve, even if it's a small one. Teams are stronger and the members are more aligned after the conflict is resolved well. For instance, and I know that you know there is no such thing as a family without conflicts—and that there is no *healthy* family without resolved conflicts. And so it goes with your relationships at work.

The next exercise is from the work of Chris Argyris, an organizational behavior researcher and teacher. In his ground-breaking work in the area of learning and defensive organizations, he gives us a tool called the Left-Hand Column Exercise.[1]

We will use this exercise to take a closer look at some human dynamics that give rise to conflicts. I'd like you to take out your notebook again. This time, we are going to examine a difficult conversation or conflict with someone you were involved with recently—an experience that was less than satisfactory. Please choose a conversation that is important to you, *not* one with a stranger at the grocery store.

Exercise 21a
Left-Hand Column

1. Draw a vertical line down the middle of the page, dividing it in half. Label the left side "left-hand column" and the right side "right-hand column." Use as much space as you need to record the entire conversation.
2. Consider your example of a recent conflict.
3. On the *right-hand side*, write what was *actually said*.
4. On the *left-hand side*, write what you were *really thinking*.

Left-Hand Column	Right-Hand Column
What was I *really* thinking and feeling?	What was *actually* said?

Exercise 21b
Left-Hand Column

When you've completed your story, answer at least these four questions:

1. Do you have any thoughts about what the *other person* might have put in the left-hand column about the same conversation?
2. How would you describe the nature of the conversation—were you overreacting or underreacting on the right-hand side compared with your left-hand side?
3. Did you withhold information? Or, did you say more on the right-hand side than you really meant?

4. What might be the possible impacts, positive or negative, of sharing your real thoughts or withholding them? How might sharing or withholding affect your long-term results and relationships?

Here are some more questions from the Left-Hand Column Exercise that you might want to think about and note down.

- What led me to think and feel this way?
- What was my intention?
- Did I achieve the results I intended?
- How did I achieve the results?
- How did my comments contribute to the difficulty?
- What assumptions did I make about the other person?
- What is the cost to *me* of operating this way?

Note: There might be times when your left-hand-column thoughts should remain private. Use the left-hand column as a resource for your own understanding and learning and make your decisions accordingly.

I hope you will bring more of your real thoughts and feelings into your conversations and relationships because the more authentic you are as a person and as a leader, the more trusted and effective you will become. There are other payoffs as well: you are likely to be less frustrated, and you just might prevent future conflicts more often.

When a conflict does arise, it's important that you have the skills and tools to deal with it well and possibly even transform it into something healthy. That's why I am going to give you six steps for conflict resolution now. Each one has suggestions within it that you can apply whenever you believe they are helpful.

I'd like you to notice that in resolving conflicts, we *inquire* (ask) first and *advocate* (tell) second, the *reverse* of what we do in constructive feedback. The primary reason for this reversal in conflict situations is that *you* need to understand what is going on immediately so that you don't blunder into assumptions. Another reason is that emotions are often elevated during conflicts, so it's important for you to get them understood and calmed as quickly as you can. It may seem like we lose much of our rational brain when we're "hot" and letting our emotions rule the day. That's because we do, even without even knowing it. Use these six steps to begin to reshape and reframe your thinking so that the next time you have a conflict to deal with, you have a tool to help you resolve it.

SIX STEPS OF CONFLICT RESOLUTION

1. Recognize the emotions of the moment—yours and theirs (inquiry, then advocacy).
   - Sincerely *ask* how the other person is feeling, and listen deeply and carefully.
   - Calmly describe how you are feeling, using "I" statements.
   - Let the other person know why it is important to you to resolve the issue.
   - If you are standing, sit and invite the other person(s) to sit as well.
2. Briefly describe the problem in neutral rather than emotional terms no blame, judgment, or assumptions, and state clearly your positive intentions for resolving the issue (advocacy and inquiry).
   - Come to a mutual understanding of the current problem and establish what value resolving the conflict has for each person involved.
   - Use constructive feedback skills in describing your view of the problem and to avoid laying blame.
3. Use deep listening skills to truly understand the other person's point of view (inquiry).
   - Say that you know you may not have all the facts.
   - Ask open-ended rather than yes/no questions to bring out critical information and issues.
   - Keep seeking and listening until you both completely understand the conflict and each other's point of view (mining).
   - Confirm your understanding by paraphrasing and summarizing.
   - If your new understanding means that you need to apologize, do so sincerely. If it means that you still have a conflict, keep working to resolve it.
4. Share your perspective of the problem (advocacy).
   - Use what you have learned from the other person to help define the problem.

- Without blaming or "you" statements, let the other person know your perspective and what you need and/or want.
- Share what the impacts of the conflict are for you, and what they appear to be for the other person or for others who may be affected.

5. Work together on a positive plan of action to resolve the conflict (dialogue).
   - Agree upon the issues that need to be addressed and share responsibility for implementing a resolution to transform the conflict.
   - Make a plan together and identify the next logical steps in the plan.
   - Share responsibility for implementing the plan.
   - Document the what, who, and when, including follow-up dates to check in on progress.

6. Summarize and express appreciation (inquiry, then advocacy).
   - Summarize what you believe has been accomplished and your agreements.
   - Share how you feel about the progress.
   - Ask what progress the other person believes has been made.
   - Appreciate the other person's efforts, and thank the person for working through this conflict with you.

It's a good idea to review these six steps regularly; you might even print them and hang them where you will have a handy reminder. *Practice is key.* Each time you resolve any type of conflict, you will become more confident, there will be fewer people who you cannot look in the eye, and you will be a much better leader.

There are many different "flavors" of conflicts. Identifying the root cause of a conflict at the beginning of the conversation is helpful. If you don't know, you will need to use the six steps to uncover it.

TYPES OF CONFLICT

Interpersonal Conflict

Interpersonal conflict occurs when people have different goals, values or beliefs, needs or wants, or they wish to behave in ways that are opposed to cultural norms. These conflicts can erupt into all kinds of arguments that can get serious, such as political differences, labor versus management, parents versus children, among team members, within friendships, and so on. Emotions tend to run high and hot in interpersonal conflicts, and relationships are mended or broken depending on the outcome. Example: *Ted and Mary are a couple. Ted believes that Mary's churchgoing makes her a religious puppet. Mary believes that going to church is expressing her spiritual freedom and is greatly offended. Ted and Mary will need to resolve their conflict if they are to continue as a couple.*

Informational Conflict

Informational conflict occurs when different facts, figures, or expert opinions are at issue. Sometimes people can look at exactly the same information and interpret it very differently. Assumptions can get in the way of the facts as well. Example: *The project team must make a report to the CEO. Eric, the team leader, insists that the facts demonstrate a clear upward trend, while Catherine is positive that the data demonstrate a negligible growth steady state. Eric and Catherine must resolve their dispute before they can make their report.*

Procedural Conflict

Procedural conflict occurs when there is a plan, but the steps (1, 2, 3, and so on) are not clear and there are different opinions about how to get to the goal. Example: *Ten people have volunteered to help raise money to build a new seating area for clients in the outreach office. Everyone knew the goal, but no one knew who was in charge, the priorities, and who was doing what by when. There were wildly differing opinions about the priorities and time line. The group must resolve their conflicts to move forward.*

Group Development Conflict

Group Development conflict occurs when the ground rules and behavioral expectations have not been made clear and/or agreed upon by the group, with the result that problematic behaviors begin to emerge. If some people want to jump straight to the task and others want to make sure that everyone has a say in every decision, there will be conflict. If the meetings are not run well, there will be conflict. If the wrong people are at the meetings, conflict will erupt. Example: *The task team was given a problem to solve; they agreed on the facts and agreed on the definition of success. Their charge was clear. However, there was no appointed leader, so they anointed the first person who spoke. No ground rules were set up, and people began wandering in late and fiddling with their mobile devices. Several people stopped showing up and didn't let anyone know. This team needs a "do over" to establish ground rules and then stick to them. They need to determine how they will make decisions and who has what roles. They must resolve their conflicts or they will not finish well.*

While there are others, these four types of conflict are the ones I see most consistently in organizations and on teams. They often leak into one another. It's not uncommon to have interpersonal conflicts arise out of any of the others, or to have something that looks procedural develop into a group development conflict. In fact, I've even witnessed all four operating at the same time! This isn't pleasant for anyone, and it can be difficult to unravel in some cases. However, when the conflict(s) is (are) resolved and good practices are put into place and maintained, the results are well worth the effort.

As with constructive feedback, this conflict resolution tool will not solve all conflicts. Part of learning about one another and growing together involves our slogging through some conflicts and coming out the other side, maybe a bit muddy, but alive and stronger.

History, egos, and lines in the sand can divide people. For some, hanging on to *my way* or *my stuff* can be more compelling than working to find what is in the best interest of the whole or for the greater good. Conflict can transform to collaboration, or at least détente, when people can understand and respect each others' points of view. People can move on with a fair compromise. They don't really move on if they believe they've capitulated, given in, or given up.

There are times when you may walk into an explosion that you never saw coming. I call this *spontaneous conflict*. As with spontaneous combustion, you have to put out the fire before you can find the cause and clean it up. You'll notice that many of the six steps for conflict resolution still show up.

TIPS FOR SPONTANEOUS CONFLICT

Deal with Emotions First—Always

When people are exploding with emotion or rigidly stubborn, *stay calm, keep your voice low and clear*, and deal with emotions first. Recognize and legitimize people's emotions. You can reduce the level and heat of emotions by acknowledging them and seeking to understand: "You seem/are upset; what's going on?" Then listen carefully. Give the person a good long chance to diffuse her emotions. Most people want to be heard and understood. If they need to cry, let them cry, or if they need to pound the table, let them pound (as long as they don't damage it). They will wear themselves out if you give them a chance to vent without interrupting them or stopping the flow. Be patient and empathetic. Do not get sucked into the emotions of the situation yourself.

Control the Physical Setting

Again, in any conflict, control the physical setting and do your best to insist that people who are standing, sit down. Go get chairs if you need to. Get them off their feet. If this happens in a public place, move to a private place as fast as possible. Really insist on this—walk away if you must, saying that you are not going to have or allow this conversation in the open. It's harder for anyone to "save face" when he's imploded in public, so help him get out of there—even if the conflict is aimed at you.

Keep It Small

Include only the people who are part of the conflict, not passersby or others. If it's a group conflict, break the group into pairs or smaller groups and allow them to discuss the situation with a clear instruction to talk together to share what they see or feel is going on—what the conflict is and why it has broken out. Let things get quiet, and then, one by one, assuring no interruptions, ask each person how he or she is feeling.

Listen

No matter what the size of the group (a group is two or more people), set up ground rules for behavior and roles, so that respectful listening can occur. When people aren't listening to one another, intervene and ask them to clarify or paraphrase what others are saying and feeling before they add their own comment. Such a structure will often reduce emotion and allow for mutual understanding.

Reverse Roles

When you ask people to imagine that they are walking in the other person's shoes, it creates an opening for empathy and allows each person to break down those absolute positions. When you are negotiating a situation in which not everyone can win and only one or two ideas can be used, have people argue for a solution other than their own. Quite often one idea will rise to the surface.

Now that you have all these tools and information, it's time to practice resolving a conflict that you have in your life right now. I'm going to walk you through a process to help you identify what that conflict is and how you can best deal with it. Please use your notebook for this exercise.

Exercise 22
Conflict Practice

From your experience, write down a conflict situation or problem that you have with another person that you need to resolve. This should be a real conflict that you are facing or, if nothing is looming, one that you have faced recently. If you do not have a work-related problem, use one from your personal life. Take enough time to develop and describe the problem in detail, and then come up with solutions and a plan.

- List who is involved.
- Give a full description of the problem/conflict situation.
- Identify the known causes of the problem/conflict and do your best to identify which type of conflict it is.
- Describe your desired outcome or objective.
- Using the conflict resolution tool and all 6 steps, determine your best approach and possible solutions.

I hope that you were able to fully work through a conflict challenge of your own and come out the other side with confidence. If you run into a block or two, enlist someone you trust to help you think about the situation as objectively as possible and discover options that you may not have already considered.

Leaders are often called upon to resolve conflicts between two or more people, perhaps between their own direct reports, perhaps between another leader and your direct report, or some similar situation. In the event that this happens to you, here are a few steps to help you facilitate a conflict between people:

PROCESS FOR SUCCESSFULLY FACILITATING CONFLICTS

Prepare a Short Agenda

This lets everyone involved know that there is a structure to this meeting, and there are expectations of sharing information and coming to some resolution.

Lay Out your Ground Rules of Engagement

Ask all the parties if they can agree to live by those rules. Do not proceed unless they agree.

Check In

Ask all the parties how they feel about being there. Listen and acknowledge emotions and feelings from all parties.

Reality Check

Ask all the parties how they felt just before they went home yesterday. (This gets at the tension level and helps them see that their pain is shared—as it usually is. It also makes this a personal story, not just a work story.)

Set a Goal(s)

Ask what is the *one* thing that must happen today if each of them is to feel that this meeting has been successful. (Write this down to revisit at the end of the meeting.)

Identify Areas of Agreement

Ask participants to spend a few minutes to write down their answers to the following questions and then ask each person to answer without interruption, one question at a time:

- What are three things on which you believe all parties agree?
- What are the real problems as you see them?

- What responsibility do *you* accept in relation to the problems?
- What would a positive outcome look like to you?

Agree to an Action Plan

Write down specific who, what, when, where, and how next steps in the process that each party can live with and that will make a difference in their relationship going forward. There must be measurements to allow each of them to know whether the plan is working or not. All parties must make a verbal commitment to address the conflict again if does not remain resolved.

Bring Closure to the Meeting

- Get the parties to take personal responsibility for follow-up.
- When each has acknowledged his role in the conflict, ask what behavior(s) he or she will agree to change to improve the relationship.
- Review the desired outcome of the meeting and ask how close you came.
- Remind all the parties of their vulnerability to repeating behavior that is harmful to positive outcomes. Ask them to immediately address any further tension or conflict and act to resolve it quickly.
- Ask them if they feel better now than they did when they came in.

In the event the situation gets out of control at any point—that is, if the exchanges become repeatedly heated or if there are few, if any, areas of common ground—the facilitator must make a judgment call: to redirect the discussion and proceed, or to table the discussion until all parties are able to come back and work on it again. In the latter case, make another date as soon as possible. It is better to close down the discussion for a time than to make the situation worse. *Never* continue if you feel that you cannot handle the situation.

It is important for each party to be able to safely vent her feelings about the problems and to own responsibility for them. Insist that the parties use one another's names rather than "he" or "she." Keep good notes, and if there seem to be misunderstandings or lack of communication, you should interject and paraphrase what each person said. Keep working with them to make sure that the messages are clear and that each person's important points are heard and understood (not necessarily agreed with). Referring back to the areas of agreement is always helpful because most people will find more areas of agreement than disagreement—much to their surprise.

You (as facilitator) are not the *fixer*, but rather a neutral party, the clarifier and referee. It is essential that the facilitator say as little as possible while guiding the parties down a path of mutual understanding. This may need more than one session—a time-out of sorts that will allow both parties to integrate what they have heard and felt and to come back fresh to the second session. Schedule the next session for a few hours later or the next day, but do not wait a week. Keeping up the momentum and coming to closure as soon as possible are important to success.

We've covered a lot of ground, and I'm sure you can see how fundamental deep listening, constructive feedback, and conflict management skills are if leaders are to be able to guide, coach, and develop their people effectively and create healthy and thriving organizations.

At your fingertips, any time of the day or night, you now have access to the deep listening techniques, the six steps for constructive feedback, and the six steps for conflict resolution as well as facilitating conflicts. You can redo the exercises as often as you like for new situations. Scribble, bookmark, tag, or do whatever you need to do so that you have what you need handy when you need it.

There is no shortcut or magic to making these skills part of yourself and your style. This is the real deal—you have to want to integrate them into your life if you are to make it happen. The great news is, everything you need in order to do it is right here, including *you*!

We could look at the topic of conflict for years, and many people do. From my perspective, what it boils down to is having the courage to deal with our garden variety daily conflicts using fairly simple and proven tools. These will get you well on your way. Now you just have to do it—and I know you can.

KEY LEARNINGS FOR INTERPERSONAL MASTERY

1. Interpersonal mastery skills are directly related to Emotional Intelligence competencies and to a leader's success.
2. The three dialogue skills of deep listening, constructive feedback, and conflict management are core skills that will help you increase your interpersonal mastery.

3. All our work happens through people—one relationship and one conversation at a time. When the conversation stops, the relationship stops.
4. Successful dialogue is a two-way process; what people hear is what matters, not what you say or what you think they *should* hear.
5. We are not leading if we are not listening, and we are not listening when we are doing anything else.
6. To listen deeply, we need to emphasize our *focus* and *attitude* toward the other person.
7. It may be a paradigm shift to consider constructive feedback a gift.
8. If you are managing up, you are managing your career; if not, you're not.
9. It may be a paradigm shift to understand that conflict is a necessary and healthy part of any relationship.
10. In any conflict, always acknowledge emotions first.

PART 4

TEAM MASTERY

Chapter 14

TEAM MASTERY

Never doubt that a small group of thoughtful, committed people can change the world. Indeed, it is the only thing that ever has.
—MARGARET MEAD

Definition: Team Mastery is having and utilizing the skill sets and the Emotional Intelligence competencies necessary to successfully guide a group of people with a shared purpose to their desired goal.

Leaders who want to succeed need to have their teams succeed. Period. Of course, teams are made up of individuals. You remember I said that people and groups are messy. So it goes with teams. It takes awareness, attention, time, and skill to get the best from our teams. And it's worth every ounce of investment.

Any enterprise, whether it's for-profit or nonprofit, relies heavily on teams to do important work. Teams may be long- or short-lived, depending on their purpose and their success. They may focus on the big picture or on a specific task, outcome, or goal. Regardless of why a team is formed and who is on the team, the practical "how to's" of building and maintaining an effective team do not vary much at all. It's also clear that those teams that succeed have a shared purpose and have high performance standards. The irony is, most leaders know all this, but they still don't apply it. It takes time and commitment to build a great team, and a lot of people simply don't make doing so a priority investment. That's a problem.

The first step in helping teams to become high performing is to understand exactly where they currently are in their development process, and then identify where they want and need to go next.

In their book, *The Wisdom of Teams*,[1] Jon Katzenbach and Douglas Smith shared their research on the direct relationship of team performance to organizational performance. There is really no question but that one begets the other. This is a book that is worth reading if you want to delve more deeply into what high-functioning teams can do for you. The real question is how to convince leaders and organizations to do the work it takes to truly invest in their teams and get those great results.

In our discussion of team mastery, we will take a fresh look at how groups and teams work, and what happens when they don't work. It's no accident that sports teams have won championships even when they have far less talent than their competitors. The primary reasons they win with less talent are:

1. Their leader values and insists on true teamwork.
2. The team members are committed to one another's success.
3. Their leader believes in and supports them in good times and bad.

A big differentiator between high-performing teams and everyone else is that they maximize the talent they have for their shared purpose. This creates a result that is far greater than the sum of their individual contributions. I expect you know this instinctively. We have all seen or been a member of teams that work and teams that don't. We know the difference.

I'd like you to make a list in your notebook of the things you instinctively know about effective and ineffective teams. Draw a line down the middle of the page and write "Ineffective Teams" on the left side and "Effective Teams" on the right side. Below each heading, write the characteristics and behaviors of each from your experience and perspective.

Exercise 23

Ineffective Teams	Effective Teams
1.	1.
2.	2.
3.	3.
4.	4.
More?	**More?**

It would be easy to say, "OK, just stop doing everything on the left and start doing everything on the right," but I know it's not that easy.

Let's make a quick "diagnosis" to see where you score your team(s) so that you can begin to understand how well your team is operating right now. For each of the 20 statements in Exercise 24, place a rating number by the description that best describes your team. If you lead or are a member of more than one team, copy the exercise and do it again for each one. Please answer these questions as you think you actually are today, not as you would like to be or think you should be.

Exercise 24
20-Question Team Health Check
Rate Each Question from 1 to 5

1 = Not at All   2 = Rarely   3 = Sometimes
4 = Often   5 = Very Often

1. Ground rules of behavior are agreed upon, and all members are accountable to them. _____
2. Meetings are regularly well run and an effective use of everyone's time. _____
3. The leader of the team is known at each team meeting (even if it varies/changes). _____

(Continued)

4. The leader's expectations of the team are well understood. _____
5. Team members' expectations of each other and of the leader are clear. _____
6. The team's purpose/charge is clear to everyone. _____
7. Roles and responsibilities of each member of the team are clearly understood. _____
8. Everyone knows how his or her work fits into the "big picture." _____
9. Team members have the opportunity to work on interesting and varied tasks. _____
10. Everyone knows how each decision will be made within the team. _____
11. The team members share a common mission, vision, and values. _____
12. Team communication methods are known by all and utilized. _____
13. Team members are aware of team development stages and challenges. _____
14. Morale on our team is high. _____
15. Team development is viewed as an important and ongoing team goal. _____
16. Team effectiveness and member commitment are measured and addressed regularly. _____
17. Conflicts are readily addressed in accordance with team ground rules and values. _____
18. Team members receive constructive feedback regarding their performance. _____
19. Each team member takes personal responsibility for her or his actions and behaviors. _____
20. Team members do a good job of balancing individual and team needs. _____

A score of 4 or 5 on any question indicates the team is on track in this area.

A score of 3 on any question is an area needing your attention sooner than later.

A score of 1 or 2 is a red flag needing your attention and intervention immediately.

It is a wise leader who asks the team to anonymously answer these questions and then shares the results and works to address them.

The challenge for leaders is to avoid the trap of relying on hope, prayers, wishes, or miracles to create stellar, high-functioning teams. Getting great results happens on purpose and by design. It is a big part of every leader's job to build teams that work, that utilize the organization's time and resources well, and that achieve their intended goals. Once again, too many people think it is easy for teams to get their work done—just give them a charge and a timeline and let them at it. Too often, I hear leaders and team members say things like, "We don't have time for that stuff—we have real work to do." Nothing could be further from the truth! You are wasting time and resources by not doing the real work of consciously building your team.

In the following chapters on team mastery, I'll provide several useful tools, models, and activities that you can put into practice immediately to help you assess and improve your team. While I am not suggesting that these are all that you need in order to build good teams, these six elements are always involved and, when they are used, will have a significant impact on your team's success.

1. *The stepladder of group dynamics.* This model will help you understand and work with the key elements of any group's dynamics from the ground up.
2. *Mission, vision, and values.* We will define the mission, vision, and values for the team and the organization. In our discussion of personal mastery, you did this for yourself. Here, we will discover how to create compelling, meaningful words to live by in your teams and organization.
3. *Decision making.* It's the why, what, who, how, and when that matter in decision making. By the end of this chapter, you will have discovered how to create practical decision-making protocols that are easy to live with and live by.
4. *Delegation.* Those who have been individual contributors and are now leaders often find that delegating is difficult to do. Delegation is a mindset as much as it is a process.
5. *Meetings that work.* Teams need to meet to get work done; they need to communicate and interact, discuss, and decide. Most people have too many meetings, and many of them don't meet the needs of the people who are attending them. We are going to solve that problem by focusing on simple ways to ensure that your meetings are effective instead of a waste of time and money.

6. *Trust building.* A solid foundation of trust is at the core of all successful relationships. Learning to build trust on purpose, and with a purpose, is not difficult. Since no relationship, no team, and no organization will go far without trust, we'll look at ways to be more purposeful about building it. If *all* you do as a leader is build trust with people every single day, you will be utilizing nearly every skill set in this book.

As you can see, team mastery is a very meaty subject, and it has to be. We get our work accomplished with and through others every minute of every day—so we need to get it right.

If you still have any doubts about the importance of this topic, or if you muttered to yourself that this is all that "touchy-feely" stuff, think again. What happens in teams falls directly and quickly to your bottom line, and everyone, no matter what your business may be, has a bottom line. Profit or nonprofit, we all have revenues, expenses, credits and debits, customers, stakeholders, and reputations. The relative success or failure of your teams will have a huge impact on how positive or negative your bottom line will be, and on what people believe about you, your team, and your organization.

Now that I have made the case for team mastery, let's get at it!

Chapter 15

THE STEPLADDER OF GROUP DYNAMICS

It is better to have one person working with you than three people working for you.
—DWIGHT D. EISENHOWER

You may wonder whether there is any difference between a "group" and a "team." It's a good question. The following works for me when either a group or a team asks for my help.

A group is made up of two or more individuals who have one or more specific common interests, and who may or may not share a mission, vision, and values or have a shared identity as a group. They may come together for one specific reason, such as a specific event or to accomplish a particular task. Examples could be people marching together for a cause, volunteers collecting toys for kids during the holidays, a classroom, a faculty meeting, or a department of people who are loosely connected.

A team is made up of two or more individuals who share a common mission, vision, and values. They identify as a team working toward shared goals. When a team is effective, its members have a strong sense of team identity, and they all know that they are interdependent—that none of them alone can achieve their shared task, goal, or vision. They hold themselves accountable, and all members have roles and responsibilities within the team. Examples could be a project team, a team of lawyers or doctors working for the same client's well-being, a sports team, or even a couple or family.

Neither is better or worse than the other—they simply work differently and have different dynamics and purposes. The key for you, the leader, is to determine what you need to have and to then ask, "Is our group or team being effective for what we want or need?" Here, our focus is on teams.

Some of you may have heard of Bruce Tuckman's four-step Team Development Model,[1] where the steps are Forming, Norming, Storming, and Performing. These are good descriptions of what is taking place within the stepladder, but they don't tell the whole story.

The stepladder model of group dynamics is based loosely on American psychologist Abraham Maslow's hierarchy of needs, a theory arguing that human psychological health is predicated on fulfilling innate human needs in a given order of priority.[2] The focus here is on both the team and the individuals within it. You might think of team maintenance the same way you think of car or home or personal relationship maintenance. If you take any of them for granted, and assume that it is just fine because you haven't heard any bad noises or bad news, you are asking for a heap of trouble down the road. No oil, no engine!

You'll notice that in Figure 15.1, the stepladder graphic, every group or team begins with a shared purpose, the reason why they are together. Let's look at the steps, one at a time.

1. *Safety.* The first step is creating safety for each team member. This is about asking, "Who am I in the team?" Do I belong here? What influence can or will I have, what role do I have, and what contribution can I make? Will people listen to me? This is the beginning of how groups are formed and the entry point for any individual. Those questions must be answered to our satisfaction or we won't be able to move on. We each need to feel physically and emotionally safe and to know the rules of the game (also called group norms), so that we can move to Step 2, trust.

2. *Trust.* Trust asks the question, "Who are you?" of the other members of the group. We need to know whom we can trust and how other people think. For each of our teammates, we will ask ourselves whether we can count on this person to do her or his part. Do I trust that conflicts will be handled well? Once we have trust in our

Figure 15.1   The Stepladder Model of Group Dynamics

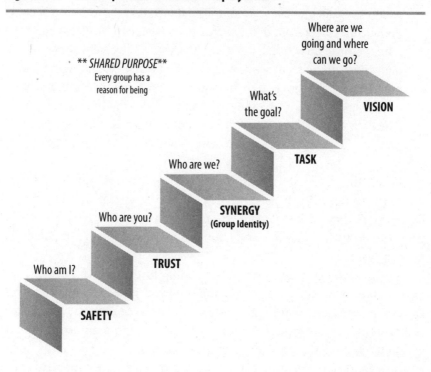

SHARED PURPOSE
Every group has a
reason for being

Where are we
going and where
can we go?

What's
the goal?

VISION

Who are we?

TASK

Who are you?

SYNERGY
(Group Identity)

Who am I?

TRUST

SAFETY

teammates, and that includes the leader, we can begin to form a sense of group identity and synergy.

3. *Synergy.* Synergy, or group identity, is about learning the answers to "Who are we as a group?" and How do we identify as a whole? How can we best work together and complement one another's talents, interests, and styles? The group then begins to identify which role each person will take on and how the group is going to accomplish its work.

4. *Task.* This is the performing stage. The focus is on the task or goal, and it asks the question, "What is the goal?" The answer should be aligned with the reason the team was brought together in the first place. Because we are all well versed in the art of getting tasks done and we've been rewarded for it all our lives, we often *jump* to the task before we've learned how to work well together. Once we know who we are as a group, we can do a far better job of tackling the tasks we are supposed to be working on to reach our goals.

5. *Vision*. We started with a shared purpose. Now that we have learned what we're capable of and accomplished our task, the question is, "Where do we go from here?" Some teams come to closure at this point because their task had a clear life span. Conversely, some high-functioning teams continue for many years, even though their membership changes and their shared purpose evolves. At this step, teams need to revisit why they exist and decide whether there is a benefit to staying together. If there is not a reason to stay together, they need to bring the team to closure consciously and gracefully.

Where do you suppose most teams and groups begin on the stepladder? You are right if you said Step 4, task. You've seen it so many times, haven't you? This is called *jumping to task*, ignoring entirely what motivates people to do their best work and failing to make sure that each person is fully engaged.

When we *jump to task* without attending to the first three steps, we do so at our own peril. It's a lot like building your house on a foundation of sand or even quicksand! Ignoring the first three steps on the stepladder demonstrates a clear lack of Emotional Intelligence in a number of areas within the social awareness and relationship management quadrants, such as organizational awareness, teamwork, inspirational leadership, and conflict management.

It's important to note that the whole team is as high or low on the ladder as it's *lowest* member would place herself. Think about it. If even one person is not feeling safe enough to speak what he sees as the truth, or does not trust the entire team for any reason, the whole team will reflect that reality. You get the best from your team when you get the best from each and every member, not just some of them.

The stepladder can be, and often is, dynamic rather than linear; it depends on the people and events. We often are working on more than one step at a time simultaneously. Conversely, at any point, a team may need to stop and rebuild. Whenever there is a disruption, such as a conflict or a membership change, the team will need to return to the foundational steps in order to get back on track and check in with its members. The leaders and the members need to determine, not assume, how any changes have affected them. Ignoring events that change or affect the team and its members is an oversight that will cost the leader and the team time and results.

Too often, leaders and team members perceive the first three steps as a big waste of time. "Just do it—get on with the job—hurry up—we're not here to play games and make everybody feel happy!" Have you ever heard those words before? Have you said them?

Ask yourself, when was the last time you saw a miserable team succeed? I rest my case!

I call the stepladder the *pay now or pay later* model. When we jump to task without building a strong foundation, we may find that we've jumped over a cliff. Yes, we did it really fast, and it was a great cliff jump, but seriously, do you really want to go over that cliff without someone on your team holding a strong safety net? And no one will be, because your team members are not invested in you or in the team's success.

This is not spectacularly insightful of me; it's common sense. It is simply our human hierarchy of needs playing out in our teams. These needs do not disappear when we throw people together; they are *magnified*.

You keep hearing me say that people are messy and groups are messy! Still, as leaders, we have to learn how to get the best from our people and our teams. You will be able to do that a lot more successfully when you make the upfront work a conscious priority. This work *is* a task in itself—it's a *group maintenance task*, and it must be attended to if you want to create high-functioning teams. The stepladder is a great model to help guide your efforts.

Here's the bottom line wake-up call: when we do not invest in building a strong foundation of excellence in our teams, our house falls down. Or if it stands, it's wobbly, and it takes us double, triple, or even more time to complete our tasks and clean up the conflicts and problems that inevitably arise. This means that time invested in your teams up front is *smart business* because we get our tasks completed *faster*, *better*, and *cheaper*.

Let me be really clear. The objective is *not* to build country clubs at work. The objective is to build high-functioning, highly productive teams that get outstanding results.

STEPLADDER TEAM ADVANCEMENT TIPS

Safety

- Plan for introductions and warm-up activities.
- Establish ground rules or rules of engagement and decide how you will enforce them. A "code word" that is humorous is

often helpful. Examples: "lemons," "time out," "dragon breath," and so on.

- Ask about and understand everyone's hopes and concerns for the team.
- Discuss the skills, roles, and responsibilities needed.
- Understand individual interests, knowledge, talents, and skills.
- Use humor appropriately—never at anyone's expense.
- Honor the absent—don't talk poorly about people who are not present.
- Use round robins that go all the way around the group, leaving no one out.
- Use check-ins and wrap-ups or debriefings.
- Remember food and refreshments—don't underestimate this!
- Consider the space. Is it people friendly? Does it have windows, decent chairs, and is it private?

Trust

- Inclusive versus exclusive—there should be no cliques.
- Decide how to decide.
- Agree upon roles and responsibilities.
- Share explicit mutual expectations.
- Share personal preferences and styles.
- Share strengths and weaknesses.
- Show respect for different views and styles.
- Be candid and tell one another your truth respectfully.
- Deal appropriately with conflicts as they arise.
- Commit to individual and group accountability.

Synergy

- Develop commitments for personal contributions.
- Run effective meetings.
- Keep everyone well informed.
- Conduct team-building activities and learn together.
- Plan for shared fun, positive, "winning" and celebratory experiences.
- Create rituals, including how you welcome new members and say goodbye when people leave the team.

Task

- Establish very clear expectations of individuals and the team as a whole.
- Be explicit about how you will ensure group and individual accountability.

- Use team members' interests and skills.
- Engage the larger system as needed.
- Identify timelines and milestones.
- Use project management skills.
- Celebrate accomplishments!

Vision

- Decide how or whether to continue, change, or end the team.
- Create a shared vision for the future, if this is appropriate.
- Be creative and passionate about what is possible.
- Use what you've learned to build an even stronger team.

Let's make this real for you. Take out your notebook and draw two copies of a stepladder similar to the pictures in Exercise 25. Then answer the questions in the exercise in your notebook.

Exercise 25
Where Is Your Team on the Stepladder?

1. Think about your *primary* work team—the people who *you lead*. Think about how each person participates, each person's body language, and comments made. Take a *guess* about how each member of your team (including you) feels about being on your team and where the members might place themselves on the stepladder. Put team members' names next to each step.

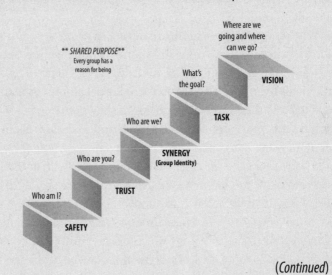

(Continued)

2. Now think about a team in which you are a member but *not* the leader. Place *yourself* on the stepladder for that team or group and think about *why* you put yourself there.

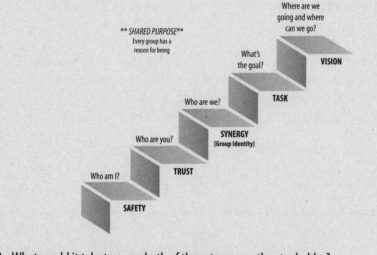

3. What would it take to move both of these teams up the stepladder?

I mentioned ground rules or rules of engagement in creating safety within a group. Doing this is one of the most important, and the least considered and remembered, component of building and continuing a successful team of any kind.

Why do you suppose ground rules are so necessary? You are right if you said that without them, time and money will be wasted because if people don't feel safe, they will not be fully engaged. This critical activity allows individuals to express and create shared expectations, establish norms, and begin to build the culture of the group as they need it to be. Without ground rules, trust is more difficult to establish and maintain, again, costing time and money down the road.

Always make the time to create ground rules with and for a new group. It's easy to make this happen with a new group or team. With an established team, a way to approach it is to simply tell the group that it's important to take a *temperature check* from time to time to understand what's working in your meetings and your work together and what could improve. To that end, you'd like to set aside some time on the next agenda (so that the members can think about it and it's not a surprise) to get explicit about your ground rules, rules of engagement, or operating principles (use whatever term you wish) and to make sure that everyone is on the same page by the end of that discussion.

Really, it's not hard. One of the most interesting things I do when working with any intact team is to ask whether they have any ground rules. The answer 98 percent of the time is, "No, not really." I make sure we create them.

I ask the group members to individually write down "What ground rules will encourage *you* to fully participate in this group, to feel safe, to feel like you belong, to have a voice, and to feel valued as a member of the group?"

The team members get about three minutes to think and write on their 3 by 5 card, and then I ask them to pair up or create a triad so that no one is put on the spot—more safety—and have one person report out for the group. They don't have to come to a consensus or choose. After about five minutes, we get the ground rules up on newsprint.

Confidentiality is a common ground rule for groups and teams who have work that requires it or in a training course. I help them define confidentiality to mean, "I can speak about my experiences, thoughts, and ideas to anyone, but I cannot speak about yours outside this group without your explicit permission." I then ask the group members to categorize their lists into themes to help them assess what is really going on. It's a bit like getting a diagnostic printout on team dynamics! Depending on what happens, I have been known to completely change the plan for the day because what the team members said they needed in the planning phase was clearly not what they actually needed. They have told me as much in their ground rules results.

When the day came for Paula's team retreat, I knew that something was amiss from the moment the team members walked in—just from their body language. When I did the ground rules activity with them, it was crystal clear. This team was not happy or even a team; in fact, its members were fearful. They did not want to talk about anything personal, and they worried about retribution. There was clearly a deep divide between Paula and her staff. So much for a fun-filled team-building day!

We took a break. It was then that Paula filled me in on some serious issues between herself and her team. Better late than never, I suppose! I redesigned the entire day and repurposed other parts of the plan. Had I not done so, we might as well have sent everyone home. In the end, I was able to help the team understand why there were a number of communication issues, and identify some strategies for

(Continued)

addressing them. Without the ground rules activity to help them and me understand the issues that had been unspoken and "under the table," the day would have been a disaster for everyone.

Before making assumptions or going too far in planning what you would like to do to build your team, refer back to Exercise 24 for your Team Health Check List in Chapter 14. That should give you a good idea of where to focus your energy and time.

KEY TEAM ROLES

Teams may have all these roles or only one or two of them, and you may even choose other roles that are not listed here. I offer these as a guideline and to help you think about what roles you have created or may wish to create.

Leader

This person is either officially given this role or chosen by the other members of the team to serve as team leader for some period of time. This person leads the team to successful execution of the team's charge, assignment, or task. Designation of the leader may be based on role or expertise or even rotated as determined by the team, but should not be based on who speaks first or the loudest!

Facilitator

This person moderates the group process. This person is not the decision maker and has no "skin in the game." This person makes sure that the group process stays on target and points out issues that may be derailing the group. The leader can also be the facilitator, but it's not easy to do both and focus on the group's task along with the group's process for achieving this task.

Timekeeper

This person is in charge of making sure that the group stays on time with the agenda. This could also be the facilitator, but it can help to have another person keeping track of time spent on agenda items or any other time-sensitive matter.

Recorder

This person is in charge of taking notes or minutes for the group and is effectively recording the *group memory* to make sure that ideas are not lost and agreements and decisions are documented for the team.

Process Observer

This person is responsible for observing and reporting on the team's process, including participation of members, task focus, relationship development, creativity, group harmony, and other such factors. This could be the facilitator, but it can be useful if someone is managing the logistics and someone else is managing the human interactions.

Jester

This is generally a self-appointed position. This person helps the group to keep a sense of humor and finds ways to keep people from taking themselves too seriously so that stress does not get out of hand.

Responsibilities are different from roles. Someone may take on the process observer role this week, and that same person may also have the responsibility for researching the history of payments to Company X by your next meeting.

As we continue with team mastery, more puzzle pieces will begin to fall into place. It is indeed a puzzle, one in which the parts often have minds of their own!

Chapter 16

TEAM MISSION, VISION, AND VALUES

The bottom line is that leadership shows up in the inspired action of others. We traditionally have assessed leaders themselves. But maybe we should assess leadership by the degree to which people around leaders are inspired.
—DR. JACK WEBER

Mission, vision, and values in teams and organizations are the maps for you and your people to follow so that everyone is moving in the right direction. The concepts involved in doing this work on a larger scale are exactly the same as the ones you used in your work with your personal mission, vision, and values.

In my work with executive teams, I often help them create new vision statements for their organizations. One of the biggest traps for leaders is to confuse vision with mission. Another common mistake is to lump vision together with a laundry list of strategies and tactics. We're going to clear all that up right now so that you can better guide your teams and organizations. You will be able to create explicit statements and send clear messages about each important part of the mission, vision, and values journey.

Definition of terms:

Mission is our purpose—it's why we exist, do business, and it describes exactly what we do.
Vision is our passionate dream for the future—we're not there yet, but we are deeply committed to getting there.
Values are our promise—how we will conduct ourselves while executing on our mission and advancing toward our vision.

It is the leaders' job to establish mission and vision for everyone else. It is important that values are developed with input from all those who must live by them. So let's say you work for a widget company, Widgets Inc., and your mission on the wall says, *"We Make Widgets."* That is exactly what you do. It is why you are in business. It is your purpose.

Your vision might be, *"We will be the number one widget company in the world."* If that is your vision, you will make very different decisions from those you would make if your vision were, *"We will create the widgets that change the world."* The former could be something that Jack Welch might have said. The latter could easily have been the mantra of Steve Jobs. You do see the huge difference, right? Both are fine clear visions, but they are very, very different. Each will drive choices and behaviors in profound ways.

Moving on to values, let's say that your widget company's values are integrity, excellence, respect, and teamwork. These examples are mom and apple pie values, to be sure, so bear with me. They also are completely meaningless if they have no teeth or accountability measures to accompany them. They are a painful reminder if they are just slapped up on the wall so that you can say you have values!

On the flip side, if they have teeth and buy-in from the people whom they affect, these simple values can completely define the workplace culture. For each value word, (and I highly recommend limiting your list to the top five or fewer, or people won't remember them), you need a short definition so that everyone is absolutely clear on what you mean. For instance, for integrity, you might say, *"We do the right thing—even when it is difficult."* Now everyone knows generally what you mean by integrity. You will then explain it even more with examples.

Within each value must be observable and measurable behaviors for which every person in your widget company, including the leaders, can and will be held accountable. These must be clearly articulated. Within integrity, you might have five to ten behaviors such as, *"We keep and follow through on our promises,"* or, *"We tell the truth."*

These have meaning and clout when and only when the values are incorporated into the fabric of the organization. They must be part of recruitment and hiring, position descriptions, performance management tools, and training and development.

When leaders are held to the same standards as everyone else, or even higher standards, your values have meaning. Only then can you say that you are a principle- or values-based organization. Anything less is smoke and mirrors. I'm sure you have heard this question, "Do you walk your talk or just talk the talk?" This is all about values. The bottom line is: Do you say what you mean and then do what you say?

Imagine a world at work in which everyone is on the same page—you know what your mission is, you know where you are going, and you know how to behave along the way. Everyone is expected to focus on the same big things. It's a whole lot easier to paint all your people and their jobs into your organization's picture when these are all very clear and aligned.

Being clear about mission, vision, and values is not quite enough, though. We need to drill down a bit to get to the meaty bits. Strategy and tactics are not your mission or vision, and they aren't the same as each other. Leaders often get confused here, and therefore so do their people.

Once you've become clear about your mission, vision, and values, the work of getting those things accomplished needs to begin. You need strategies and tactics.

Let's define these terms.

Strategy is our focus—those significant few things, not 57 things, that we will do to measurably advance us toward our vision, with a timeline and the appropriate resources to make it happen. *They must align with our mission, advance our vision, and be in harmony with our values.* These become our top priorities because they are our best, biggest, and current plans for moving our business forward. Some people refer to these as Big Hairy Audacious Goals (BHAGs). Call them anything you like (call them boulders or gorillas or mountains)—as long as they are the truly significant big things on which you will focus and that will help you advance your vision. Then…you're good to go!

Tactics are our actions, or smaller, laser-focused objectives; they are those activities, work plans, and events within various parts of our organization that, when accomplished, will achieve our big strategies.

For instance, your widget company may have a key strategy that says you are going to buy up every other widget company you can find and bring them all up to your standards. This strategy is directly aligned with your vision to "become number one in the world."

Your tactics, on the other hand, are much closer to the actual work. You might assign an associated tactic to a particular division of your widget company. Maybe the group is asked to analyze balance sheets of every company in the world that makes widgets so that you can report to senior leadership exactly what you believe it will take to purchase each company.

A summary of all these elements for Widgets Inc. is given in Figure 16.1.

Figure 16.1   Widgets Inc. Example

Mission: We make widgets.
Vision: We will be the number one widget company in the world.
Values: Integrity, excellence, respect, and teamwork

1. Integrity: We do the right thing, even when it's difficult, by:
   - Keeping and following-through on our promises
   - Admitting what we don't know
   - Creating consequences (positive and negative) to acknowledge performance
   - Sharing our mistakes and problems, and learning from them
   - Telling the truth
2. Excellence:
3. Respect:
4. Teamwork:

Strategy: Buy up widget companies that will help us grow by 30% in the next 3 years.

Tactic: Analyze the balance sheets of every widget company in the world.

While you are buying up widget companies, you need to do it within your well-established values of integrity, excellence, respect, and teamwork that you and your employees agreed upon. This means that if you *could do* a shady deal and make a lot of money, you won't do it—because *values trump vision.*

We've all seen plenty of examples in which the reverse was true, where the end justified the means for some very high-placed "leaders" and their followers and where the value "greed" trumped the espoused values. Some of these people are no longer in charge, have lost their companies, and some of them are in court or in jail. It's good to remember that your organizational values will broadcast your character far and wide. Sooner or later, if you act in opposition to your espoused values, a big ripple, perhaps as strong as a tsunami, will come crashing back full force and bite your credibility and reputation in tender places.

Now, it's time to revisit the great vision test. Remember, a great vision has to pass all four criteria that we discussed in personal mastery, if it is to get you where you want to go.

Is your organization's vision:

Inspiring. Is your vision worth committing everyone's time and life force to?
Clear. Does your vision create a clear picture of your desired results—one that everyone can understand instantly?
Credible. Will your vision stretch the sense of what's possible and still be believable—do you and your people believe that they can do it?
Commitment. Is your vision more than a good idea? Does everyone believe that this is the right direction, and are they committed to do whatever hard work it takes to get there?

Take a look at Exercise 26 and write down your organization's current overarching mission, vision, and values, if they exist, if you can find them, or if you remember them. If they don't or you can't, there's definitely work to do! If you don't know and/or you can't find out, I'd like you to imagine what they should or could be by using the definitions of each I listed earlier.

If you are a leader of a team, even if that team is just you and one other person, write down your team's current mission, vision, and values. Surprisingly many teams have not gone through this process together and then wonder why they are having difficulties being focused or collaborative or *on the same page.*

Exercise 26
My Organization's Mission, Vision, and Values

Our mission:
Our vision:
Our values:

My Team's Mission, Vision, and Values

Our team mission:
Our team vision:
Our team values:

Working without mission, vision, and values is a lot like taking a road trip without a map. You will get somewhere—but will it be where you want to go? Doing this work with your team will give you the opportunity to reinvigorate your people, get them excited about what they are doing and where they are going, and provide them with guideposts along the way.

Keep in mind that you should also be able to answer a resounding *yes* to each of these three questions:

1. Do we hold ourselves accountable for our carrying out our mission?
2. Do we hold ourselves accountable for advancing our vision?
3. Do we hold ourselves accountable for living and modeling our values?

In the next chapter, we will explore the topic of decision making. You, your teams, and your organization will make many important decisions in creating a mission, vision, and values. How you go about decision making is often as important as the decision itself.

Chapter 17

DECISION MAKING

It's not hard to make decisions when you know what your values are.
—Roy Disney

Decisions, decisions, decisions—we have to make hundreds if not thousands of tiny and big ones every day. We have to decide when we get up, what to wear, what to do, and where to go, and that's all before our first cup of coffee!

At work, decision making is an integral part of everything we do, and yet many people, teams, and organizations have few, if any, decision-making protocols that map out how decisions will be made, by whom they will be made, what method will be used, and finally how decisions will be communicated.

One of the first things I do when I begin to work with a client is to ask a wide variety of people, from the top all the way through the organization, how decisions are made. The answers speak volumes about the leaders, their values, and the culture. Decision making is a big deal; we all know this from our own experience. It's important that we do it well. So how do we do that?

It's easy. Really, it's easy. I bet you never thought you would hear that, but it is true. Let's take a look at why it's true.

In your personal life, what drives your decisions? Think about it carefully. What makes you get up, get dressed, brush your teeth, and get to work on time? The answer is—your personal mission, vision, and values. It's true; you do all these things without even thinking. This is true even if all you know is that a part of your purpose is to put bread on the table, and therefore you want to keep your job, or at least *a* job. In addition, you want to be presentable at work. Those basic thoughts drive your actions, and your thoughts are driven primarily by your values, with your mission and vision coming in a close second.

The same is true when you arrive at work. Your decisions are based on your values and your organization's values, whether you are consciously aware of it or not. We rarely give this much thought, and therefore we rarely make the connection between our values and our decisions.

Mission and vision also drive decisions at work. For example, let's go back to Widgets Inc. It would make no sense at all to make a decision to make airplanes if your purpose is to make widgets. And it would make no sense at all to ignore big talent gaps when your vision is to become the number one widget company in the world, and when you espouse the value of excellence. Once again, mission, vision, and values play a big part in what you do and how you do it.

Now for the easy part. Once you have those key elements in place, there are five questions that you need to answer:

1. What is the decision that needs to be made?
2. Whose decision is it?
3. How will we decide? What method(s) will we use? This is often referred to as deciding how to decide.
4. When must the decision be made?
5. How, when, and to whom will the decision be communicated?

Let's take these questions one at a time, using a single example to illustrate the point. Imagine that you've just learned about a widget company in Australia that looks promising. You also know that it's far away and that you have no people or facilities there. All this new information gets the decision ball rolling.

Using the five questions will help us decide.

What's the decision that needs to be made? If you can articulate it, you know the answer, and if you can't, you don't. So begin with a lot of clarity. Look for related decisions within the larger decision. For instance, there may be competing priorities to consider; there may be cash flow, political, and timing decisions involved. Make sure you know all the decisions that need to be made, not just the big, over-arching one. Map out the decision to see how many touch points are affected by a simple "to buy or not to buy" decision. *Be explicit.* What exactly needs to be decided?

Whose decision is it? If you have decision-making protocols established, this should be easy. Protocols define who makes which decisions, and that person's or group's authority level. It is critical that you know this and communicate it up front. Are you the decision maker? Is this a group decision that you will not override? People don't usually mind what the answer is, but they mind a lot if you've already made the decision and are pretending that it's still up for discussion. Let's say you have protocols in place, and your board of directors and CEO make all acquisition decisions. There's no confusion; it's crystal clear. If you have no protocols in place, you need to create them before you do anything else.

How will we decide? Again, this is easy *if* you have protocols in place. Perhaps your board and CEO have bylaws that require a two-thirds majority for certain spending levels, or perhaps it has to be a consensus decision, where everyone has to be able to both live with it and support it. Whatever method you choose must make sense for the type of decision and the risk involved. For instance, you do not need unanimous board approval to buy toilet paper for the restrooms, but you might need it for buying companies.

When must the decision be made? The timing of the decision may be driven by internal and/or external factors. Normally the designated decision makers also determine the timing of the decision. They may ask for input and consider a number of perspectives; still, in the end, the decision makers own the "what" and "when" outcomes. It is important to know and share the timeline for the decision so that the impacts of the decision can be managed well and people can get on with their work. Taking too long or not long enough can be frustrating and create unintended and even dysfunctional outcomes.

How, when, and to whom will the decision be communicated? This question is often overlooked, and yet the success of a decision depends to a large extent on how well that decision is communicated. Consider who needs to know, who is the messenger, how it will be shared, and through what means—in person, by e-mail, or over a loudspeaker. Often the choice of messenger sends a message of it's own—is it you, the team, your boss, or the board? It will feel very different to the receivers depending on who sends the message. Communication also includes a decision-making process, and it should become an explicit part of your protocols.

Decisions can be made quickly, efficiently, and by the right people for the right reasons at the right time. There is little or no confusion when everyone understands decision-making protocols and decision rights. When I explain to leaders that this whole process can happen in 30 seconds or less, they can't believe it. Then they see it happen almost effortlessly. Of course the up-front protocol work, and those decisions, had to happen first, but it is definitely worth it. This quickly becomes a bottom line issue because of the huge amounts of time and energy that are routinely wasted (or not), opportunities that are lost (or not), and resources that are well utilized (or not). When everyone knows the what, who, when, and how to make the decision, we know that the leaders are leading.

Decision making happens too often at work to leave it to chance. And, by the way, making no decision *is* a decision. It's a tactic that can be either constructive or destructive, depending on the person and the situation. Without clear protocols, you need to answer the five questions one at a time each and every time. Still, as long as you do a good job in answering the questions, you may be able to prevent the "who's on first" syndrome.

Making too many ad hoc or reactive decisions is simply not a good business practice anywhere. Frustrations about micromanaging or, conversely, benign neglect leadership can occur because leaders have failed to put clear decision-making protocols in place. When people know where their "fences" are and how big their "sandbox" is, they understand what decisions they can/should or can't/shouldn't make. When they don't know these things, a low-risk or even a no-risk–high-fear culture is likely to fester and grow. Giving people clear decision rights helps them grow, learn, and understand that their decisions have real consequences. This, of course is as true at home as it is at work.

It's wise to drive as much decision making to those closest to the work to eliminate unnecessary bureaucracy and bottlenecks. Are you a "fast company/organization" with clear and sensible protocols, or do you slog through 10 signatures to buy toilet paper? Do you have an operating reality of *touch it once*, or a reality of *keep touching it until it screams*?

Laura was approached by a member of her staff just before the end of May. Bob wanted to know if he could work four 10-hour days and have Fridays off from June through August. Laura's response was step back, look at the bigger picture and ask Bob to help coordinate all summer flextime in the office to make sure that everyone had a voice in the decision about his or her own schedule. She told Bob the "givens" about minimum staffing and the hours of operation. Other than that, Laura left all decisions to Bob and the group, asking him to give her the schedule results with everyone's names and plans. Bob was a little nervous, but he took it on because he really wanted to have the flextime he requested. Some people didn't want to change their hours, and some people did. Within the framework Laura provided the group could make a consensus decision that all seven people in the office could support.

There are four main categories within the Decision-Making Protocol Worksheet (see Exercise 27):

Type of Decision
Level of Risk: High-Medium-Low
Knowledge Needed: High-Medium-Low
Authority/Job Level/Name: High-Medium-Low

Here are two examples of protocols for two different kinds of decisions. What they have in common is they are both about human resource decisions.

HUMAN RESOURCE DECISION PROTOCOLS

First Decision

Type of Decision: Final hiring approval for professional staff in Department XYZ.

Level of Risk: High. A bad hire is very costly in every way—financial, morale, and productivity.

Knowledge: Medium. The person needs to know how to oversee a professional, legal, and successful search and ensure that the right people are on the search team.

Authority: High. Department head final decision—currently Pat Smythe.

Second Decision

Type of Decision: Summer flextime schedule in Department XYZ

Level of Risk: Low. If it doesn't work, it can be quickly changed.

Knowledge: Low. Need to know which staff are needed for what time periods.

Authority: Low. The team is delegated to make the decision based on the department head's parameters of staffing needs and office hours, and then report the plan to the department head.

Use your notebook to make a grid for yourself. For this practice, consider *one* and *only one* category of decision with multiple levels of responsibility. Is it a project, financial transaction authority, purchasing, operating policies—you choose and create your matrix of protocols based on the level of risk and the knowledge needed. Consider the various levels of decision making within this topic area, and who will make those decisions.

Exercise 27
Decision-Making Protocol Worksheet

for _____(i.e. Human Resources, Finance, Project X, Legal…)

Type of Decision	Level of Risk	Knowledge Needed	Authority/Job Level/ Name
	High-Med-Low	High-Med-Low	High-Med-Low

Sometimes we do not realize what went right or wrong with a decision unless we take the time to examine it more closely. Take a moment to think about a decision you made recently that went very well and another that did not go well. Take the time to really think about what worked and what didn't work in each case. Use those insights to consider an upcoming decision to make sure that you apply what you've learned from your own experience.

TYPES OF DECISION MAKING

Not all decisions are equal. Therefore, the leader, and sometimes the team, must evaluate the situation, the people, the relative impact, and the positives and negatives of various decision-making methods before making each decision. Each of the methods listed is valid and can be valuable at different times for different reasons. Effective and skilled leaders know when to use each for the greatest overall gain.

Autocratic

The leader makes the decision. This is a valid method as long as it is clear from the outset that the leader will be making the final decision, with or without input.

Inclusive

The leader gathers input from others before making the decision, but she isn't looking for a recommendation—just input to inform her decision. Never pretend that input matters when it doesn't. Everyone will sense this, and the leader will lose trust and credibility. The leader retains the power to make the final decision.

Participative

A group makes a recommendation that the leader will almost always honor, but the leader retains veto power if he cannot live with the result. Recommendations should rarely, if ever, be vetoed if the group understands the boundaries, the givens, and their scope, given the subject matter. Communication between the group and the leader must be handled well. This method helps to create significant buy-in and commitment to the decision by all parties.

Democratic

One person, one vote. Majority rule. Or a two-thirds vote, or a quorum, or whatever the agreed-upon numbers of votes needed to carry the decision may be. The leader retains no veto power in this method.

Consensus

Everyone has to be able to live with and support the decison. The key here is that the right people are having the discussion; no one is being "railroaded," and everyone's voice is fully heard. The leader retains no veto power in this method.

Delegated

The decision is delegated to those that it affects the most, and the leader retains no veto power or even attachment to the outcome.

No Decision

No decision *is* a decision; it is a decision not to decide. Do this consciously, not because you are avoiding having to make a decision when one is needed. The power to choose this type of decision making is determined by the decision maker(s) for that decision (see above).

DECISION-MAKING METHODS

When more than one person is involved:

- Unanimous = 100 percent agreement. This would only be used when it is a group decision of some type above when the leader does not retain veto power.
- Voting = whatever numbers are agreed upon to carry the vote. Used with group decisions.
- Multivoting = votes can be cast for multiple choices and then often the majority carries, or two-thirds, or whatever is chosen. Used with group decisions.
- Consensus = everyone making the decision has had a voice and agrees to both live with and support the decision. Used with group decisions.

Rather than just having people raise their hands to vote or shout out yay or nay, I have found it helpful to use the "Rule of Thumb" voting method, particularly for consensus decisions and definitely for unanimous decisions. It's even helpful before taking a majority or some other kind of vote, to help people understand what's still on the minds of those whose voices may not yet have been heard. Here's how it works:

A Voting Tool: "Rule of Thumb"

- It's not a vote unless every person who is present votes.
- Decide up front whether you can vote without people who are not present and whether anyone not present is bound by the vote of the rest of the group.

The way thumb voting works is as follows:

Thumbs up = I'm 100 percent on board
Thumbs sideways = I have a thought or a concern
Hand raised = I can't decide until my question is answered
Thumbs down = No way; I cannot support this action

In the case of thumbs sideways and thumbs down, you must pay attention and learn what is on people's minds. Check it out—ask the person what she is thinking, and be open to listen. Make sure that everyone has the same mental model of what you are voting on. Ask: "What would it take to change this to something that you can live with?" Allow the group, and not just the leader, to be involved with the question. Be willing to table the decision to allow more time to think and gather information if needed.

Do not publicly attack or judge someone who is in opposition. That person may have a thought or a perspective that is crucial to the question. At the very least, each person's voice needs to be heard so you know what's on people's minds. "Group think" or "agree with the boss" to keep him happy, are not behaviors you should want to encourage.

Decisions matter, and how you delegate decision-making authority affects the success of the work you want to see accomplished. In the next chapter, we will examine what delegation really means; it may surprise you.

Chapter 18

DELEGATION

No matter what accomplishments you make, somebody helped you.
—ALTHEA GIBSON

Let's start with a simple question: What do you think delegating means? Is it assigning tasks, or perhaps giving work away? Maybe it's getting rid of things that you really don't like to do. If that is similar to your experience, we have another paradigm shift to make. While leaders have every right to assign work and give work away, delegation is something else entirely.

*Definition: Delegation is a planned and well-managed **new** learning opportunity for another person that transfers duties and/or responsibilities to that person for a mutually beneficial purpose.*

Many leaders (in fact, most leaders with whom I have worked) have some or a lot of difficulty with delegation. They freely admit this and worry about it. It is, after all, the leader's responsibility to develop her people. This often is not made explicitly clear when you are called to become a leader, but count on it: it *is* an important part of your job.

In our lifetime, the need for developing and coaching employees has exploded at all levels of the organization, across technologies, demographics, and rapidly changing customer expectations. Being skilled in delegation is no longer a bonus. It's an essential leadership skill.

Today, it is everyone's responsibility to learn *and* to teach. At all levels, we learn from one another; in fact, about 70 percent[1] of our learning takes place on the job. We must be able to share knowledge and skills in order to increase our organizational effectiveness and capacity. It's all part of the knowledge revolution that we see all around us.

With this seismic shift in roles must come an equally large shift in *mindset*. Delegating is one of the biggest mind shifts that you will need to make when you become a leader.

Let's take a look at new ways to think about and create delegation opportunities.

Delegation can be up, down, or sideways. Does that surprise you? When do you think it is smart to delegate up? How about when the task requires more authority or influence than you currently have? What about delegating sideways? This is a good idea when the task requires different skills, experience, or knowledge from what you can or have time to offer.

Now, how about delegating to people who report to you? This is the primary focus of the delegation chapter because it's your job as a leader. Delegating to direct reports should happen when you want to develop your people, they want to learn, and/or when you are ready to let go of something, even something you love to do.

This is not *dumping* work on people, assigning more of the same to their plate, or failing to do your own job. It is *new work* for the person you are giving it to, and you should have a win/win reason for doing it. You might think of it this way: delegation is more like teaching someone to sail the boat than assigning him to the task of bailing water. Anyone can bail water; sailing is a skill.

A big part of why you are where you are right now in your life is because other people thought you could do it. Someone encouraged you and gave you a chance. That had to happen just for you to get hired in your current job. All your life, people have been delegating new things to you to help you grow your knowledge and skills. I guarantee it. Can you think of how many people have given you a helping hand, taught you something new, or believed in you?

Let's go down memory lane for a moment. I'd like you to remember a time when someone trusted you with a job or task that you wanted to learn. Remember how she let you do it yourself and then let you call it your own. Please take out your notebook and answer the six questions in Exercise 28.

Exercise 28
Delegation Questions

Remember when someone trusted you with a *new* job or task:

1. What was that job or task?
2. Who delegated it to you?
3. Why did that person delegate it you?
4. How did you feel when you were first learning it?
5. How was that different from when you mastered it?
6. What did that person gain by delegating this job or task to you?

My goal is to have you remember how great it felt to be trusted, because now *you* are the teacher who must find the time and motivation to trust the people to whom you delegate tasks. It's time to *pay it forward*!

One of the biggest success stories of my life and my career is about delegation. No matter how much I loved leading and facilitating our leadership development program, I couldn't be "it" forever, and I knew I shouldn't be. This was my baby, and letting anyone else lead it was beyond scary. Still, a one-woman show was not sustainable, and I wasn't setting a good example for delegation. I took the plunge and created a facilitator training course and process. By the time I left the organization, we had more than 20 people who could do all kinds of programs, including leading my three courses.

That was 20 years ago. Today, most of the people I trained are leaders now and are facilitating outstanding programs and teams, teaching others how to do the same, and doing just as well in their own way as I did in mine. It was a big lesson for me about the positive and far-reaching impact that delegating well can have.

Take out your notebook for Exercise 29. It is intended to help you think much more deeply about what you can actually delegate.

Exercise 29
Delegation Truth Telling

Things I have delegated	Things I could delegate	Things I'm uncertain about delegating	Things I cannot delegate

---

I hope you really put yourself to the test with this. Revisit it again in a day or two and really challenge yourself concerning things in the "uncertain" and "cannot" delegate categories. Brainstorm on your own and with others you trust to unearth new ways in which you could actually delegate more to gain benefits for you, your people, and your organization.

If delegating makes so much sense, what keeps us from doing it more often? If you are hanging on and delegating little or nothing, the first question I would ask you is, "What are you afraid of?" Is it sharing knowledge, job security, thinking no one can do it as well as you can—what? If you are afraid to delegate, then you are afraid to lead.

Maybe it's something else. What blocks *you*? Could it be a time problem, there is no one to delegate to, you don't trust anyone else to do it, or maybe you really like the task or get great strokes so you don't want to give it up?

It's time to choose—are you a leader or an individual contributor? Either is fine; just don't confuse the two—they are very different jobs with different expectations. Leaders delegate.

A quick search on the Internet will result in dozens of various delegation models. They have a lot in common. I suggest that you find one that resonates and works for you. It really doesn't matter which model you use to keep yourself and your delegate on track; it matters that you *have a model and use it.*

I use these 10 principles. They have worked very well for me as a leader for decades. I am one of those people who love to delegate! Maybe it's because I get bored easily. I prefer to think it's because I derive a lot of satisfaction seeing other people get excited about learning new skills. In any case, I will continue to do whatever I can to work myself out of a job and pass my knowledge on to others. It sets me free to learn and do all kinds of new and interesting things.

10 PRINCIPLES OF DELEGATION

1. **Select the right person**. Choose someone who is capable of doing the task and who is the right person at the right time. Consult the person before you delegate. Delegation flows both ways. Let your delegates participate in determining what is delegated to them.
2. **Show and tell.** People learn by doing more rapidly than they learn by just being told what to do. People have different learning styles; consider theirs, not yours.
3. **Delegate good and new work.** Delegate interesting, rewarding, and challenging projects to increase motivation, commitment, engagement, and development. If you give others just your dirty work and tiresome chores, you will get the opposite results and toss in resentment as well.
4. **Take your time**. Your delegate will need time to acquire the training and expertise that she needs to handle everything that you might want. Be realistic about how much time is needed for her to learn *and* become proficient.
5. **Delegate gradually and monitor progress carefully.** If you have been underdelegating, don't try to transfer too much responsibility overnight. Take your time, be thoughtful, and plan. If your delegate is new to the job, don't expect him to immediately assume the same amount of responsibility as others on the same level who have been with you longer or have more experience. Situational leadership theory is operating here.[2] Different people will be in different places

on different learning curves. Include that reality in your plan before you delegate anything to anyone.

6. **Match authority with responsibility**. There is nothing worse than having all the responsibility and no authority to make sure that the job gets done. Do not hamstring your delegate with a mismatch of responsibility and authority. By empowering employees who perform delegated jobs with both the responsibility and authority to manage those jobs, leaders free themselves to manage more effectively and at a higher level of effectiveness.

7. **Delegate the whole**. When this is possible, delegate a complete project or action to one person rather than giving away just one little piece of the action. This will give your delegate the full picture, control and coordination of the work, and cut down on confusion and errors. Expect, and even hope for, mistakes. Allow the person room to innovate if possible, and try new things; they might find new and better solutions.

8. **Delegate for specific results**. Instead of describing to your delegate the scope or way to do the job, describe the specific results that you expect.

9. **Avoid gaps and overlaps**. A gap is a job or part of a job for which no one has been assigned responsibility. An overlap is a situation where two or more people have responsibility for the same job. Bad things will likely happen in both situations.

10. **Trust the successful delegate**. Now, let the person you have delegated to do it. From now on, he makes the day-to-day decisions, and has a free rein to use his own resourcefulness within the boundaries you have established. Your job now is to appreciate and reward your successful delegate!

Put your plan in writing, if only so no one forgets anything important. I suggest that you create your own delegation worksheet based on the 10 principles and anything else you want to include. In the meantime, use Exercise 30 to practice. If you pick a delegation model from the dozens available, simply abridge the worksheet to suit your situation. If you are delegating to a team, simply replace the word *Delegate* with the word *Team*.

Exercise 30
Delegation Worksheet

Name of Delegate: _____

Name of Delegator: _____

Delegated Job/Task: (describe in detail)

Authority Granted Delegate:

Time Frame: (training, practice, take over)

Milestones:

Communication Plan:

Performance Standards:

Risk Factors:

Resources needed:

Plan Agreed to: Delegate _____ (signature)

Delegator _____ (signature)

Date: _____

In the final analysis, you don't even have to be altruistic about delegation. Go ahead—be selfish! There is a huge *what's in it for you* story here. Over time, you will achieve higher efficiency, increased motivation, deeper bench strength, and better distribution of work throughout your group. Best of all, you will be free to do new and different work that you never had the time to explore before. With all this information, I hope you are inspired and well on your way to becoming a star delegator!

Chapter 19

MEETINGS THAT WORK

If you had to identify, in one word, the reason why the human race has not achieved, and never will achieve, its full potential, that word would be "meetings."
—DAVE BARRY

Guess how many hands go up when I ask any audience the question, "How many of you look forward to the meetings you attend?" You are right if you said, "Very few if any." Most of us have too many meetings and most of them don't function well. In fact, all the research tells us what you already know instinctively: at least 50 percent of the meetings in our country are a waste of time and money. If all your meetings are in the happy 50 percent that work, by all means skip this chapter; you've got it nailed! If, on the other hand, you are frustrated, exhausted, and annoyed by many or most of your meetings, then let's fix that for you right now.

I'd like you to stop and take a really close look at the last one or two weeks of your actual work calendar. Then answer the five questions in Exercise 31.

Exercise 31
Evaluate Your Meetings

1. How many meetings did you have? Count them.
2. What percentage of your week was taken up by meetings?
3. How many of those meetings were you looking forward to? Why?
4. How many were you dreading? Why?
5. What percentage of your meetings would you say were a good use of your and others' time?

There *are* meetings that I'd never want to miss. People need to congregate, network, learn, collaborate, decide, discuss, exchange ideas, mind-meld, team-build, brainstorm, and have fun together.

If we put dollar signs instead of hours on our meeting calendars, we might think twice. A one-hour meeting with six people who average $60,000 a year in salary and benefits costs a company about $175 per hour. That's a *very* conservative calculation. Once you add prep time, travel, space, technology, follow-up time, and any assistance for setup (see Figure 19.1), you can double the cost to $350 per hour!

We need to get our money's worth. Otherwise, why have an expensive meeting. If at least half of the meetings we attend are a waste of time, then a lot of our human capital is, well, flushed down the toilet. If we were to add up everyone's costs in every lousy meeting in the United States in one year, we would have enough money to buy a small country, or at least a big island, because it adds up to billions (that's billions with a *B*). I think that's a compelling enough argument for having well-planned, well-executed meetings, don't you?

Figure 19.1   Formula for the Cost of Meetings

1. Estimate and add together the total annual salaries (*S*) and benefits (*B*) of all attendees.
2. Divide the answer to Step 1 by the number of people in the group to get the average $*S* + *B*.
3. Divide the average $*S* + *B* by 2,080 (= 40 hours a week × 52 weeks) to compute the average hourly rate per person (AHR).
4. Multiply the AHR by the number of people in the meeting to get the cost of each *hour* of that meeting.
5. For a truer real cost that includes all the indirect costs, double your answer.

I'm reminded of the Thomas Kayser quote, "Time and money, money and time, with respect to meetings they intertwine, and when all the costs are added up it blows your mind."[1] Point well taken! Wouldn't it be a good idea to quantify the value of your meetings, or if not the value, then at least the cost of them? I have used this formula with many teams, and it never fails to shock people when they see how much money is spent on meetings. The next time you are in a meeting, try it and see what you discover.

Here's an idea. Suppose you place the amount of cold, hard cash that each meeting costs you in the middle of the table. Put two cans on the table: one to burn it in after bad or wasted meetings, and one to invest in whatever you like after the good meetings. Would that get anyone's attention? Would it get yours?

Ever since meeting researchers started keeping track in the 1950s, we have been meeting for more hours every year. It's a bit like global warming: it creeps up on you, and before you know it, your life is one big meeting desert or tsunami or both, at the same time, in the same meeting.

The way meetings are run in your organization is a result of your internal cultural norms. These come directly from the skill or lack of skill of those who are leading and facilitating the meetings. New people will conform sooner or later and perpetuate those meeting norms. What kind of meeting norms are you reinforcing? Are they healthy and productive, or not?

Since meetings can serve a lot of purposes, both great and not so great, let's evaluate yours. It is useful to look more closely at the differences between a meeting that works and a meeting that does not work. In your notebook, create a chart similar to the one in Exercise 32. Write down what you know from your own experience.

Exercise 32
Meetings That Work and Meetings That Don't Work

Characteristics of Meetings That Work	Characteristics of Meetings That Don't Work

You know the differences, right? We all do. The problem is, too often we don't change anything to ensure great meetings. Nor do we do anything to prevent hellish ones. However, we sure do complain about them to ourselves and to other people. How's that working for you? Has it solved anything?

I expect you are looking for tools that will help you now. And you won't be disappointed. Honestly, it's pretty easy once you get the hang of it. You do have to invest time up front to make sure that the meeting is going to be good. That's a fact. There is no magic bullet, but there are magic methods that will get you there. Here's some shorthand for you.

Think "PAL," where P is planning, A is agenda, and L is logistics. Answer the questions in each category, and you'll have a good shot at a great meeting.

Planning

- What are the objectives and the shared purpose for this meeting— why are you meeting?
- How will you accomplish them?
- Who will be there, and are they the right people for your agenda?
- What kind of time and space do you need to carry out your agenda?

These questions need to be considered again in the creation of the agenda and in planning the logistics and activities to work through the agenda.

Agenda

Does every item on your agenda have one of three purposes or a combination of them identified?

- *Information.* Sharing stories, important or timely information, or answers to questions. No more than 20 percent of any meeting should be spent in sharing information. There are plenty of other and cheaper ways to share information.
- *Discussion.* This requires the group to talk about an agenda item to hear people's input, views, ideas, and concerns. You need to have a method to do that well.
- *Decision.* Make a decision about the agenda item. Best decision-making practices should be followed when a decision needs to be made by or with the group that is present.

Logistics

Logistics includes all the activities and techniques that you use to facilitate the group dynamics and the meeting's flow. You want your plan and your agenda to work well, and to be a good use of everyone's time and energy. There are a number of logistics to consider: space and time, checking in and wrapping up, ground rules, food, breaks, activities, humor, use of technology, and the like. These are not small matters when you consider how much you are investing in the meeting.

I had allowed myself to be caught up in "meetingitis" for years. At one point, my projects were so big that I had no choice but to start turning down meeting requests. I cut 50 percent of the meetings from my calendar. I stopped allowing anyone, including my boss, to schedule me without my permission. It fascinated me that no one noticed at first, and my productivity and effectiveness went up. When I was asked to attend a meeting, I asked two questions:

1. What is the agenda?
2. Why do you want or need me to attend?

The answers either completely freed me from the need to attend the meeting or showed that a quick answer was all that was needed. If there was no agenda, I declined outright. *That* did get noticed. People, particularly my staff, began creating good agendas. My meeting hours stayed down by that 50 percent, and I could finally get important work done.

I'd like to share a very handy Synergistic Meeting Model (see Figure 19.2) that you can copy and hang up in your workspace. It evolved when a colleague, John Rutkiewicz, and I were teaching group dynamics and good meeting protocols to leaders. John did a great job of making what we were teaching come to life in a new way. I like this model because it effectively captures many of the concepts I've talked about here in one attractive and holistic picture.

You will notice that the goal is to help you build safety, trust, and synergy (the first three steps on the stepladder) in every meeting that you have.

Figure 19.2   Synergistic Meeting Model

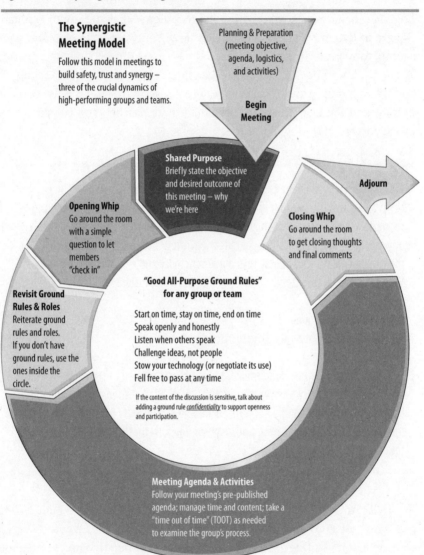

The Synergistic Meeting Model

Follow this model in meetings to build safety, trust and synergy – three of the crucial dynamics of high-performing groups and teams.

Planning & Preparation (meeting objective, agenda, logistics, and activities)

Begin Meeting

Shared Purpose
Briefly state the objective and desired outcome of this meeting – why we're here

Adjourn

Opening Whip
Go around the room with a simple question to let members "check in"

Closing Whip
Go around the room to get closing thoughts and final comments

Revisit Ground Rules & Roles
Reiterate ground rules and roles. If you don't have ground rules, use the ones inside the circle.

"Good All-Purpose Ground Rules" for any group or team

Start on time, stay on time, end on time
Speak openly and honestly
Listen when others speak
Challenge ideas, not people
Stow your technology (or negotiate its use)
Fell free to pass at any time

If the content of the discussion is sensitive, talk about adding a ground rule *confidentiality* to support openness and participation.

Meeting Agenda & Activities
Follow your meeting's pre-published agenda; manage time and content; take a "time out of time" (TOOT) as needed to examine the group's process.

If you prefer something with a more linear framework, use the bare-bones Meeting Design Planner. Let's work through it in Exercise 33. Take out your notebook to fill in the answers to the five questions in the exercise. It will work well as a framework to help you think about what to think about, and it can work well for single and relatively simple agendas.

Exercise 33
Meeting Design Planner

Instructions: Let's assume that you need to plan and facilitate a meeting with your team to share and discuss one to three things that you have learned from reading this book so far. Use the following questions to develop a plan for the meeting.

1. *Planning the meeting.* What are the goals or desired outcomes of the meeting? What is the agenda?

2. *Creating a collaborative environment for the meeting.* How will you create a collaborative environment and get your people quickly and actively involved?

3. *Structuring the meeting.* What questions or discussion methods will you use to engage the participants, steer the direction of the meeting, and facilitate group discussion and learning?

4. *Facilitating the meeting.* How will you get the group to perform the task and maintenance roles?

5. *Concluding the meeting.* How will you conclude the meeting on a high note and get the group to maintain commitments or agreements?

Each of us has the responsibility to do our part to ensure that the meetings we attend are a good use of our time. When you are a member, your behaviors and contributions are as important as anyone else's. When you are a leader and it's your meeting, the buck stops with you. How you conduct yourself and your meetings is what people will believe you want. Therefore, what you model matters.

The good news is that with planning and mindfulness, you can make substantive and positive changes. Wouldn't it be great to know that the meetings that you lead and the meetings that you choose to keep on your calendar are worth it?

The moral to this meeting story is that you, and only you, are in charge of your calendar. It's your time. It's your job. It's your life, and it's your choice. Go ahead—give yourself permission to take charge!

Building Trust on Purpose

Character is like a tree and reputation like a shadow. The shadow is what we think of it; the tree is the real thing.
—Abraham Lincoln

Trust is an outcome, not an event. Trust may form or fail to form out of our experiences (for example, "he was late three times in a row, so I don't trust he'll be on time for dinner"), or we may trust unknown others through reference trust (for example, "my best friend trusts this doctor, so I'll give her a try"), or sometimes we find it necessary to use "blind trust" (for example, "my car broke down while I was on vacation, and I have to trust the closest repair shop to fix it"). Trustworthiness for any of us depends on the degree of confidence others have in both our character *and* our competence.

Trust is a bedrock principle that affects all our relationships and our teams at work and at home, within our communities, and in government, schools, and businesses. High trust results in strengthening relationships, sustaining positive change, increasing effectiveness, and adding positive results to anyone's *bottom line*.

We all know this is true—and it matters a lot.

Therefore, growing or destroying trust is something that every leader is doing every day with each action and each comment. I would like to explore this topic with you by first raising your awareness. In Exercise 34 please think carefully about the "who" and "why" questions and write the answers in your notebook.

Exercise 34
Whom Do You Trust?

List two people who you *really* trust. *Why* do you trust each one?

1. Why?
2. Why?

List two people who you *do not* trust. *Why* do you not trust each one?

1. Why?
2. Why?

We know when we trust someone and we know when we don't. Let's go back to those people you listed whom you do and do not trust. It wasn't all that hard for you to name them, was it? It might have been a bit harder to pin down exactly why you do or don't trust them, but you could do it. The answer comes to us from our gut. Call it instinct; call it logic plus feeling; call it whatever you like.

There's more to the story.

Some of us trust first and then verify. Others verify first and then trust. This may even shift within us depending on the person and the situation at hand. For instance, I give most people the benefit of the doubt first. However, when I'm taking a risk like buying a house or a car, I prefer to minimize my risk based on previous experiences that haven't been positive. Therefore, I will choose to verify first.

Over the last 20 years, Jennifer purchased her last three cars from the same local dealer. She'd been happy with both the cars and the service. Thus, when she needed to replace her 10-year-old rust bucket, she did her research and then called the local dealer and told him what she wanted. Instead of trying to locate the car that Jennifer wanted, the salesperson tried to talk her into what he had available on the lot. Jennifer persisted, but the salesperson simply did not listen. Jennifer no longer trusted this dealership to help, to respect her requests, or to even listen to them. The character of that salesperson killed Jennifer's trust in the dealership. It took only one incident that violated her values to end her trust after 20 years of neutral or positive experiences.

Do you know which kind of person you are most of the time? As a leader, it's important for you to be aware of your approach to trusting others because you will broadcast that message without even thinking about it unless you are paying attention. Since we know that people come at trust differently for various reasons, you will need to consider what they need to hear from you, not just what you need to hear from them.

This is particularly relevant if you subscribe to the theory of situational leadership. Ken Blanchard and Paul Hersey first introduced their theory in an article on the life cycle of leadership.[1] They believe that the most successful leaders are those who adapt their leadership style to the person and the situation at hand. They suggest that leaders take into account the maturity of the individual or group they are attempting to lead or influence, and they define this as, "the capacity to set high but attainable goals, willingness and ability to take responsibility for the task, and relevant education and/or experience of an individual or a group for the task." The Hersey-Blanchard Situational Leadership Model rests on two fundamental concepts: leadership style and the individual or group's maturity level.

I agree with this as far as it goes. In thinking about delegation, how much you direct, coach, support, or delegate will depend a lot on how much you trust a particular person to deliver results on a particular task at a particular point in time. It truly is person and task dependent, and even more so if you tend to be a "verify first" kind of person.

Situational leadership does not tell us the whole story, though, does it? We also look at an individual's character and competence when we are deciding how much we trust him. You see, in deciding to trust people, we look for high levels of competence and we look for our personal definition of good character. We need to feel safe with that person and believe that he will do us no harm. Remember the importance of the first step on our stepladder.

We cannot trust until we feel safe.

We humans have been programmed since the beginning of time to pay attention to the signals that tell us whether or not we can trust someone's character and competence. In working with personal mastery, you identified the values that drive your decisions, your goals, and your vision. These all matter to you—a lot—and they all show up in your character and affect your choices that determine how competent you will be. The people around you can sense these factors in you, just as you can sense them in others.

In August 2009, after the financial crash of 2008, *Bloomberg Businessweek* magazine had a article whose first line read, "The world's financial markets nearly collapsed last fall for one reason: lack of trust."[2] Every single one of the failed organizations mentioned—and it went far beyond the financial markets—had people in leadership roles who were calling the shots, making decisions that, in several cases, affected millions of people in profoundly negative ways.

This is true on the individual level, the team level, and for entire organizations. Either people trust your individual, team, and organization's competence and character, or they don't.

No one part of our society has a corner on the market of bad leadership, that's clear! There are many examples that we can all name of businesses that had leaders who failed their organizations because they either were incompetent or had poor values and character or both. All of them violated the trust that people placed in them. In the end, this is what brought them disgrace and failure one way or another.

There *is* a ripple effect. A few, some, most, or all of the leaders in these organizations spread their influence as far as it would go, and those ripples returned and keep returning to them manyfold. This is a law of nature that won't be denied. It works whether or not the ripples we create are good ones or bad ones.

In any endeavor, we need both character and competence. We must demand both from ourselves and other leaders, and we must stop settling for and even rewarding what we do not want. For the human race to thrive, and perhaps even survive, we need to have leaders in every walk of life who are trustworthy. Really—it *matters!*

Here's the irony. Did you know that trust is also a moneymaker? In fact, it is a key innovation engine in your business, no matter what your business is—profit or nonprofit. Trust affects your bottom line, and we all have a bottom line. It also affects your sustainability. Without trust, you're out of business sooner or later, no matter how small or big you are. It follows, then, that building trust on purpose is a pretty smart idea.

When I'm teaching, I often include an activity to illustrate the huge impact that trust has on real dollars for real organizations, no matter how big or small. I stand at a flipchart with my markers. The flipchart is divided down the middle and has only two things written on it:

"Costs of Low Trust" is on the left side and "Benefits of High Trust" on the right side.

I ask people to imagine that we are writing a report for their executive director, board, CEO, VP, dean, or whomever is the Big Boss overseeing the overall welfare of their organization. Our report will provide a list telling their leader, from *their* perspective, what the impact of trust is for their organization.

Once they've answered the questions—or I've run out of paper, whichever comes first—I ask them to tell me, on each list, which of these trust items have a financial impact on their organization. The answer is always, always, always 95 percent of them. It's a huge "aha" moment for everyone! (Examples could be morale, turnover, engagement, innovation, low risk, creativity, worker's compensation, productivity, smart/dumb problem solving, turf wars, win/win, grievances, and attraction and retention of talent.)

Ask yourself, when do you actually make the time to build trust on purpose? We both know that building trust doesn't happen by accident; it requires effort and mindfulness.

In my experience, the best way to build trust with others is to *trust them*—and, of course, to do the right thing, particularly when it comes to fairness. It is a choice. Of course you have to weigh the risks as you perceive them and decide whether or not you can live with them.

We can improve and accelerate trust building. All the skills that we've talked about in the book thus far have a huge impact on trust building: the dialogue skills of deep listening, constructive feedback, and conflict management; and clarity of mission, vision, and values get your people on the same page going in the same direction. Using best practices in decision making, developing and delegating to your people, and running effective meetings *all* build trust.

I've created a series of four exercises here to help you build awareness and build trust on purpose. Please copy or write these questions and your answers to them in your notebook.

Exercise 35
Are You Trustworthy?

Be honest with yourself (no one is looking!)

1. Are you a person about whom most people would say, "I can trust him/her with my . . . (you name it: life, money, job, kids, business, spouse, sister)?"
   YES_____MAYBE_____NO_____

2. What would people say about how much they trust you?

3. Why would people say that they trust you?

4. Would anyone say that he or she doesn't trust you?

5. Why would people say that they don't trust you?

The answers to these five questions can help you think about where your gaps might be with various people in your work and home life. And, unless you are a very rare person indeed, you'll have some gaps—relationships that could use some trust building work to improve, heal, or settle them.

Exercise 36
Where Is *Your* Trust Work?

Score Yourself: 1 is low and 10 is high.

Character:

Integrity

I hold true to my values even when it would be easier not to.   _____
I take responsibility for my attitude, behaviors, and actions.   _____
I manage my priorities based on my values.   _____

Outlook

I take responsibility for my impact and my results.   _____
I encourage others and model resilience and a positive outlook
on life.   _____
I take responsibility for my own life.   _____

Gratitude and Abundance

I celebrate the success of others. _____

I appreciate and honor the wisdom and contributions of others. _____

I see possibilities and hope for the future and help others see them. _____

Competence:

Technical Skills

I am continually learning new skills so I can produce
high-quality work. _____

I seek opportunities to learn from and teach others. _____

I stay current in my profession. _____

Conceptual

I am objective about my skills and gaps. _____

I seek the wisdom of others in my decision making. _____

I am thoughtful about projects and plans before implementing
them. _____

Collaboration

I value and incorporate others' opinions and ideas in my planning. _____

I include those impacted by changes in the process of those
changes. _____

I am clear about roles and responsibilities and let others manage
their work. _____

1. Where did you score **highest** on trustworthiness?
2. How can you "model" those behaviors in your interactions with others?
3. Where did you score **lowest** on trustworthiness?
4. What do you want to do to increase your own trustworthiness in the future?

Use your answers in Exercise 36 to work with Exercise 37. This will
help take you from awareness to action rather than letting it simply fade
away. Making a commitment to work on those areas where you know you
can raise the bar on your own trustworthiness can only help you—at work
and at home. You can do this, and it's worth it.

Exercise 37
My Character and Competence Goals

From the character and competencies list:

- Circle those that you would like to focus on over the next 30 days.
- Make a list of them and write goal statements below them.
- Consider what obstacles might block you from achieving them.
- How will you overcome those obstacles?
- Are you willing to share these with someone who can help you evaluate your progress?

Character Goals
Steps I will take to achieve my character goals:

Competence Goals
Steps I will take to achieve my competence goals:

The last of the four trust exercises, Exercise 38, asks you to choose one person at work and one in your personal life with whom you'd like to increase trust. Think about all you have learned so far about MBTI preferences, Emotional Intelligence, dialogue skills, and team-building skills, and then decide which of these could help you have a conversation and take some actions that would build trust with those two people. Write down when you are *really* going to do this (yes, put a date on it). Then do it! Once you decide to build trust on purpose with people who matter to you, I'm banking that you'll like it so much, you'll keep doing it.

Exercise 38
Increasing Trust on Purpose

List two people (one at work and one in your personal life) with whom you want or need to *increase trust*
   One person in my *personal life*:

- When, what, and how will you do this?
- What might be a challenge for you?

- How will you overcome these challenges?
- What benefits will you gain from carrying out your plan?

One person *at work*

- When, what, and how will you do this?
- What might be a challenge for you?
- How will you overcome these challenges?
- What benefits will you gain from carrying out your plan?

Mutual Expectations

The last thing I'd like to talk with you about in the area of trust is mutual expectations. We know that conflicts can arise because of opposing or even poorly communicated expectations. This happens in teams quite often. We humans make too many assumptions too often! When expectations are poorly communicated, trust breaks down—sometimes in ways that are irreparable.

On the other hand, when people talk about and openly discuss mutual expectations, everything is on the table, and issues and feelings are not hidden. Whenever possible, it is useful to have someone who is not a member of the team or group facilitate this activity so that everyone involved can fully participate.

Deb, Drew, and Ruth met each other through other people. They hadn't known each other long when they created a business partnership with a handshake and one sheet of paper. It stated exactly how they would work together and deal with problems, business decisions, and money. They had no lawyers, no accountants, and no busybodies involved. They each felt that the others heard them; they shared mutual expectations and they discovered through hours of discussion and brainstorming that they had the same values and a shared vision. They trusted their instincts. Deb, Drew, and Ruth believed it was worth the risk. And, now several years later, they've proven themselves to be 100 percent right!

The Mutual Expectations Activity is a team mastery activity that is very useful in building trust and is essential to help create a high-functioning team.

Mutual expectations are those things that members of the team need and want from one another in order for them to feel successful as a member of the team. The context of mutual expectations is that these are things that may already be in place and the members of the team want to make sure continue, or they may be things that have not been discussed and/or experienced, but need to be. It's all about getting what people need from one another "on the table," so that good conversations about expectations can happen, rather than leaving them "under the table," where they get kicked around but not discussed.

Mutual expectations go beyond ground rules because they are specific to members' roles and their actual work. For instance, you may have a ground rule about not using technology in any of your meetings. Yet, when listing mutual expectations, team members might say that they really want to see minutes of the meeting within 24 hours to keep everyone on track with the team's work. This is a good time to have a discussion about whether or not the minute taker should be allowed to use technology in the form of taking notes for the minutes on his laptop.

With context and the purpose clear, the facilitator asks the team to answer these three questions and they are reported out in the same order:

1. What do the team members expect of one another? (Who answers? The team members; this is optional for the leader.)
2. What do the team members expect of you, their leader? (Who answers? The team members, but not the leader.)
3. What do you, the leader, expect of all the team members? (Who answers? The leader, but not the team members.)

Everyone answers their questions on their own and then reports out using newsprint or a smart board so that everyone can see the answers. If safety might be an issue at all, err on the side of creating smaller duos (two people) or triads (three people) to consolidate answers so that no one's answer is linked directly to a single person. Of course, the leader's answers will be known, as they should be, and the leader will go last.

You should end up with three lists with the following headings:

Team Members of the Members	Team Members of the Leader	Leader of the Members

No lists are edited or discussed, other than for clarification, as they go up. After each list is up, the facilitator should ask the team to identify themes, possibly new expectations, and manage a group discussion.

Once each list is up and discussed, it needs to be validated. Can all members of the team agree with the list of team member expectations? If not, what needs to be changed? If so, then formalize the list with a "thumbs up." Does the team understand and agree to the leader's expectations of the team? Can the leader agree with all the things the other team members expect of her? If not, why not? If so, then formalize it with words of agreement.

For instance, the team members' list may have included someone's expectation that the leader allow all team members flex-place. The leader might not be able or willing to do that, or this may not be something she believes should be an expectation, or she might need to think about it. That's a conversation that needs to happen "on the table"! It's also a good idea to get these expectations typed up and into the team's minutes and history so that they can be revisited if necessary. Slide them in right next to the ground rules.

Simply doing this activity together helps build the team and creates a more level playing field, allowing all voices to be heard. This helps to clarify and solidify the needs and hopes of all members of the team, and it builds trust—when people do what they've agreed to do.

I'd like to leave you with this summary on trust:

- Trust is the cornerstone of all relationships, and the level of trust that people have in each other is the most significant measure of those relationships.
- Without trust, you cannot succeed as a leader. With it, there are no limits to what's possible.

- The return on investment for building trust in your teams is astronomical.
- It takes time and work to build trust. It takes only a nanosecond to break it. However, the deeper the trust, the more possible it is to rebuild it.
- Trust begins with me! Indeed, it starts with each of us—first, last, and always.

KEY LEARNINGS FOR TEAM MASTERY

1. Continuously monitoring and developing your team with the five steps of the stepladder is critical to building high-functioning teams that produce outstanding results. The first three steps are often ignored, to the team's peril. Setting ground rules is critical in the safety step.
2. Mission = purpose, vision = dream for the future, values = promises to one another, strategy = priority focus, and tactics = action.
3. The five questions you need to answer when making decisions are: What is it? Whose decision is it? How will it be made? When will it be made? How will it be communicated?
4. Delegation is not dumping or assigning tasks. It is a planned and well-managed *new* opportunity for another person to learn and grow in a mutually beneficial way.
5. Every agenda item must include sharing information (a maximum of 20 percent of the time), group discussion, and making a decision, or some combination of these.
6. Your meetings cost real money.
7. Building trust begins with you and affects the quality of all your relationships; when trust is high, this can save valuable resources in your organization.

PART 5

CULTURE AND SYSTEMS MASTERY

Chapter 21

WHAT IS CULTURE AND SYSTEMS MASTERY?

Customers will never love a company until the employees love it first.
—SIMON SINEK

We began the book and this journey together by focusing on one person, you, and we then moved on to the larger group, your teams. It is now time to explore the larger systems in which you live and work and the cultures within those systems. To understand the impact of leadership, we must understand the impact of the cultures around us.

WHAT IS CULTURE?

Definition: Culture is the beliefs, customs, learning, arts, and so on of a particular society, group, place, or time. It is a way of thinking, behaving, or working that exists in a place or organization. This is a dictionary definition. I define it by simply saying, *"It's the way we do things here."*

The word *culture* is used in a number of ways to describe people: the American culture, gang culture, a culture of greed, liberal versus conservative cultures, and so on. Unless we have studied and understood the nuances of any specific culture, we can too easily fall into the trap of making sweeping generalizations and assumptions. We may assume that we know others' attitudes, motivations, values, and beliefs based on limited information and experience. Our thoughts can be infused with biases, stereotypes, and opinions. To prevent falling into this oversimplification trap about anyone or any culture, we need to ask more than we assume. We need to be open to learning from those who are similar to us and those who are different from us. This is true in our workplaces, and it's true in our world.

Let's start this journey by first learning how to assess the culture within our own organizations. In Emotional Intelligence, this helps you grow the competency of organizational awareness. Assessing your culture also gives you clues concerning what you might want to change and how. We will also explore how culture affects the systems and processes within our organizations, and therefore all the people within the system.

Culture and systems mastery begins with the premise that it is the leader's responsibility to create and nurture the desired culture within his sphere of influence. While the larger system has an impact on each leader, each leader, in turn, has an impact on it. There is no escaping this reality: as goes the leader, so goes the culture within his locus of control. Remember, it's your pond, no matter how big or small it may be. Your pond affects the other ponds, then the lakes and rivers, and ultimately the oceans beyond.

To understand systems, we need to explore the nature of change, including our common responses to change and how to navigate through them. Leading change is another organizational competency that leaders often struggle with and yet need to do well in order to succeed in moving their organizations forward. We'll explore why having a process, even a protocol, is key to having change initiatives succeed.

We'll look at the role that accountability plays within any culture and how to ensure that your systems support accountability. Accountability is a significant part of culture and systems mastery because lack of accountability will ultimately define your culture, and not in positive ways. Zero-accountability cultures and/or those with highly destructive values result, sooner or later, in shame, blame, and losing the game—no matter how big or small you are.

Finally, we need to understand the need for leadership courage within the culture and understand what it is, how to measure it in yourself and your teams, and how to grow it inside your organization. Ultimately, it's the courage to lead in both good times and tough times that differentiates the highly effective and courageous leader. This will be a leader who has both the Emotional Intelligence and the intellectual intelligence to guide her team and organization through any situation, guided by her own values and those of the organization's culture.

Why should you care?

For tens of thousands of years, humans have defined their ways of being and doing through their beliefs, traditions, rituals, values, and norms—which, of course, make up their cultures. A very basic human need is to *belong*. This makes sense because few, if any, Homo sapiens could have survived for the past 200,000 years without others helping them.

Culture has the power to give and take life. It is such a powerful force that those who are believed to have violated the norms and mores of the culture are punished in one way or another, up to and including being shunned, starved, jailed, and killed. A more positive example of the power of culture is the ways in which people celebrate those who behave in ways that their culture values highly, such as artistic creations, rites of passage, a worthwhile accomplishment, or a heroic deed. The culture may require the people within it to behave in accordance with it or risk being shunned or spit out. In some workplaces the culture may have enough flexibility to allow people to question it and work together to redefine or reshape it.

An organization's espoused culture and values may or may not reflect the reality within the organization. I am going to use the somewhat trite example of Enron here because most people know about it and understand it on some level. For illustration purposes, it is a classic and very public example of a highly dysfunctional culture.

Enron began its values statement with, *"Enron believes it has a respon-sibility to conduct itself according to certain basic principles,"* and went on to espouse its values of *"respect, integrity, communication and excellence."* The company even had the hubris to hang those values on its walls.[1]

Leaders' actions are what actually shape the culture. At Enron, the senior management made their decisions based on a single unpublished value, *"Maximize the price per share of common stock."* This wouldn't be so bad in and of itself, except that the very real subtext was, *"by any means, legal or not."* Enron's real values were, very simply, *greed-based*; that was the company's *driving principle*. This resulted in the creation of a toxic "ends justify the means" culture that made a mockery of the company's espoused values. This fatal decision on the part of Enron's management defined and consumed its culture until the company was no more.

It is a case study in *what not to do*, and it was a lesson that was incredibly, but obviously, ignored by the housing and financial sectors, which also fell prey to having deeply embedded, full-blown greed as their underlying core value. All that greed even spawned a television show about American greed!

We have all suffered from leaders who say one thing and do another. Native Peoples called this behavior *speaking with forked tongue*. The bottom line is this: one cannot overstate the importance of the leaders' role in creating, shaping, nurturing, and sustaining the desired workplace culture. I hope you can see why consciously creating healthy cultures and systems to support them really, really, matters!

Chapter 22

THE FOUR CULTURAL ARCHETYPES

A nation's culture resides in the hearts and in the soul of its people.
—MAHATMA GANDHI

Culture, as I mentioned in the previous chapter, is like the air we breathe. It is all around us, and the signs are there like the wind. Sometimes it's up there in neon lights. More often, though, there are subtle clues that tell us what's going on, and we need to look for them and pay attention.

When I teach university students about organizational cultures, they are eager to uncover the *real story* about the cultures of real businesses or groups who volunteer to be studied. One of my class teams studied a T-shirt shop in a business district that caters to students. Another team studied a trendy national-brand clothing store in the local mall. Even though they sold their goods to the same high school and college-age customers, the cultures within the two stores were vastly different.

None of this is surprising. None of this is a brilliant deduction on my part. The students, just like any of us, could sense the cultures and the differences between them, but that wasn't enough. They needed to know how to understand what was actually happening and why. They needed a method. I gave them one.

In this chapter, we will view culture through four lenses. They have different and even opposite value drivers, effectiveness assumptions, and leadership styles. The close connection to a person's personality preferences and style naturally affects the culture within the leader's influence. It is true: *wherever you go, there you are!*

Do you remember the Myers-Briggs Type Indicator that we used during our discussion of personal mastery? I built my model around the MBTI because it is a fairly straightforward way to explain the four Ps of our cultural archetypes, Product, Policy, People, and Possibility—they align with the information and decision dichotomies within the MBTI.

- Product aligns with Thinking.
- Policy aligns with Sensing.
- People align with Feeling.
- Possibility aligns with iNtuition.

The other two dichotomies, energy (E and I) and action (J and P), are present in every culture. They certainly add emphasis and nuance, but they are not the four core archetypes that drive the culture and business decisions.

When you have completed this chapter, you will be able to assess your team and organizational cultures by using the four archetypes. You will also have gained insights about how *you* affect them and how to strengthen and/or change them.

Let's take a closer look at the four cultures that dominate the world of work. As we do so, I would like to remind you that each of these cultures brings value, strengths, and challenges to the table. It is rare for only one of these to be operating within a larger organization. In fact, an organization may have all four cultures operating at the same time, but usually there are one or two that dominate and one that is the least noticeable.

Product. This is a thinking culture in which the focus is on results, objectivity, competitiveness, and transactional interactions with the external world, including customers, suppliers, regulators, and others. In a product culture, getting to the goal line really matters. These leaders are highly competitive, drivers, and all about bottom-line results. They care a lot about market share, achievement, and profits (or in the nonprofit world, influence). An example of this could be a highly market-driven company like the oil industry or United Way.

Policy. This is a sensing culture in which the focus is on control, accountability, rules, hierarchy, and formality. Attention is largely internal. These leaders focus on monitoring, timeliness, details, organizing, uniformity, laws, and rules. Examples of this culture could include government agencies and public schools.

People. This is a feeling culture in which the focus is on teamwork, collaboration, and empowerment of the people within the organization. There is a strong belief that taking care of your own will take care of everything else. These leaders care about and emphasize commitment, people, participation, service, loyalty, and teams. Examples of this culture might be Southwest Airlines or Wegman's Food Markets, and most nonprofits.

Possibility. This is an intuitive culture in which the focus is on innovation and agility. It is entrepreneurial and has few rules, with roles and priorities often shifting on a dime to do whatever needs to be done. These organizations want to stay on the cutting edge and meet or even help define customer needs with new solutions. Leaders here focus on vision, innovation, flexibility, and transformation. They even enjoy breaking the "rules" and forging entirely new pathways. Examples that leap to mind are Apple, Google, Amazon, and Zappos.

These four Ps, Product, Policy, People, and Possibility, are the predominant cultural archetypes we see in organizations around the world, not just in the United States. Next time you are out and about, pay attention and you will easily see what I mean. You'll notice the predominant culture pretty quickly. You can also check out who is leading the culture to give you more insights.

Because it is common to see subcultures within the larger culture, it's a good idea to look at both your team and your bigger system to see where they match, conflict with, or complement each other. Wouldn't you love to have a methodical way to do that? Well, fair enough; I'll give you another terrific tool.

THE C.A.T. SCAN

Let's start with four examples from the diagnostic tool I created and call the "C.A.T." scan, or Cultural Analysis Tool, and consider whether your organization is characterized *more* by:

1. Competitiveness and achievement. Is it all about winning?
2. Structure, efficiency, and control. Are rules a hallmark?
3. Teamwork and collaboration. Is it like family, and is loyalty a big deal?
4. Innovation, autonomy, and risk taking. Is it like being in a start-up all the time?

Which one or more did you choose as the main *way we do things here* for your organization? Was it Product, Policy, People, or Possibility? Was it a combination? Which one didn't you choose?

The point is, these types of culture are generally more obvious than you might have realized and fairly easy to diagnose with our C.A.T. scan (see Figure 22.1). Go ahead, take your culture for a test-drive.

Scoring the C.A.T. Scan

When you have completed Figure 22.1, you can score it. On each of the six lines within each block, list the number of points you assigned for each C.A.T. Scan heading, A through F. Total the scores in each block and then divide that number by 6 to get the average score for each culture type. This gives you a snapshot of your current culture.

Figure 22.1   The C.A.T. Scan Culture Analysis Tool

To use for organizations, substitute "organization" for "team." Spread 100 points within each set of four answers per topic

A. Primary Characteristics	Today
1. Our team atmosphere is personal. It is a lot like family. People share many aspects of their lives with other team members.	
2. Our team is very entrepreneurial. People tend to take risks and are willing to make mistakes.	
3. Our team is very results-driven. We are focused on getting the job done. People tend to be competitive and focus on their and others' achievements.	
4. Our team is tightly structured. Control is important. We have formal procedures and policies that make it clear what people are meant to do.	
	= 100
B. Leadership	
1. Our leadership focuses on mentoring, coaching, and facilitating and is genuinely interested in the development of our team members.	
2. Our leadership focuses on innovation and what could be and is characterized as entrepreneurial and risk taking.	
3. Our leadership has an outcome focus and is direct and even aggressive about results and the bottom line, for which people are held accountable.	
4. Our leadership is organized and likes things to be clear, concise, and structured. Efficiency is important, and there is little tolerance for sloppiness.	
Comments or Notes:	= 100

(Continued)

Figure 22.1   The C.A.T. Scan Culture Analysis Tool (*Continued*)

C. Style of Management	Today
1. The style of management in our team is characterized by relationship building, teamwork, getting to agreement, and urging wide participation.	
2. The style of management in our team is characterized by freedom, risk taking, asking lots of questions, exploration of possibilities, innovation, and uniqueness.	
3. The style of management in our team is characterized by achievement, driving for results, high demands, and winning.	
4. The style of management in our team is characterized by conformity, stability in relationships and in the work, having control, and creating security.	
	= 100
D. Connection	
1. The connection that holds the team together is mutual trust, loyalty to the members, and commitment to one another.	
2. The connection that holds the team together is the excitement of creativity and innovation. There is a strong commitment to staying close to or on the cutting edge.	
3. The connection that holds the team together is the ever-present emphasis on outcomes, achievement, and accomplishing shared goals.	
4. The connection that holds the team together is the structure in the formal rules, policies, and procedures. Keeping things held together well and stable is important.	
Comments or Notes:	= 100

Figure 22.1   The C.A.T. Scan Culture Analysis Tool (*Continued*)

E. Emphasis	Today
1. Our team emphasizes people and their development and success. Trust, sharing of ideas and opinions, and high participation are the norm.	
2. Our team emphasizes looking for and gaining new challenges, finding new resources, and trying new things. People who find new opportunities are highly valued.	
3. Our team emphasizes competition and goal achievement. Winning in the marketplace is a major factor in success. Hitting stretch targets is highly valued.	
4. Our team emphasizes stability and control. Keeping things predictable until there is a clear reason for change dominates. Efficiency and organization are valued.	
Comments or Notes:	=100
F. Success Criteria	
1. Our team believes that success is based on the development of people, teamwork, everyone's commitment, and caring for our team members.	
2. Our team believes that success is based on having the best products or services, being the most unique, being first to do something new, and being a leader in our market.	
3. Our team believes that success is based on getting out in front of our competition, winning in the marketplace, and achieving our goals and then some.	
4. Our team believes that success is based on being dependable, efficient, and well organized, and producing our products or services with the lowest cost or shortest time possible.	
Comments or Notes:	=100

1 = People   2 = Possibility   3 = Product   4 = Policy

ALL 1s = People	ALL 2s = Possibility
A	A
B	B
C	C
D	D
E	E
F	F
Sum of 1 responses =	Sum of 2 responses =
Average of 1 divided by 6 =	Average of 2 divided by 6 =
All 3s = Product	**All 4s = Policy**
A	A
B	B
C	C
D	D
E	E
F	F
Sum of 3 responses =	Sum of 4 responses =
Average of 3 divided by 6 =	Average of 4 divided by 6 =

You can do this again asking the question about what would be the *preferred culture* as opposed to the culture you have today. The difference in scores will help guide the work you need to do to adjust or modify the culture for the future.

There are some predictable evolutionary changes that can affect a culture; for instance, organizations can grow or shrink, or they can be affected by external factors such as demand, competition, or the economy.

As an example, the Great Recession that began in 2008 forced many nonprofit agencies, out of necessity, to become increasingly creative about funding, to collaborate more with one another, and in some cases, even merge programs, budgets, and staffs to survive. The financial pressure is actually changing their internal cultures as well as the larger nonprofit community culture.

When this happens, it is not always a bad or a sad thing. In fact, external events and pressures to change can, and often do, result in impressive innovations, new ideas, and creative solutions to old problems that no one had bothered to solve before. We have a saying that *necessity is the mother of invention* for good reason.

I am sharing these perspectives both to raise your awareness of the ebb and flow of the cultures we work within and to warn you that you should not assume that whatever your culture is at the moment will be the same in the years to come.

For our purpose here, I would like you, as a leader, to have the knowledge to assess or diagnose *what is*, the skills to *influence* what is, and the wisdom to see when what is, *isn't anymore*. Of course, I also hope you have come to appreciate the significance and impact that your leadership style has on the culture within your "pond," no matter how big or small it may be.

The next concept we will explore drills a little deeper. We now understand the four cultural archetypes operating in our world of work. Any of them can have positive and negative behaviors associated with them.

You may remember that I mentioned Chris Argyris in the discussion of interpersonal mastery.[1] He also observed what he calls Model I and Model II organizations in describing behaviors and attitudes that are either defensive or learning.

Model I: Defensive organizations foster attitudes that are:

- Controlling: act and manage the environment unilaterally.
- Competitive: it's about egos.
- Protective: of themselves and others.
- Withholding: of feelings and information.
- Attributive: and blaming of others.
- Focused: on win-lose results.
- Averse to conflict: at all costs.
- Low trust and high fear (or high distrust).

Consequences: learning and change stop.

Model II: Learning organizations foster attitudes that are:

- Data seeking: explore new ideas, take risks, innovate.
- Collaborative: people are supportive and helpful; organizational citizens.
- Empowering: autonomy and power sharing are valued.
- Open: actions and assumptions are confronted and tested; conflicts are resolved in a values-based way.
- Committed: people are engaged and take responsibility for their actions; accountability counts.
- Focused on win-win results: for all stakeholders.
- Trusting: respectful individual and organizational feedback is valued; high trust is a core outcome.

Consequences: learning and change are encouraged.

Many of us have experienced a bit, or maybe a lot, of Model I and hopefully some of Model II. Any of the four cultural archetypes we work within can be either Model 1 or Model II in the way they carry out their cultural personality.

In fact, I've witnessed a People culture that became Model I, highly insular and defensive. In it, everyone had to be *drinking the Kool-Aid*, and if an individual questioned the leaders or the culture, he was labeled as unsupportive and not a true believer, and was soon spit out—which, of course, means fired. The reality is that this was a pseudo-People culture, but there was no telling the company that!

Conversely, I've seen a Policy culture that was so rule-driven that there was very little room for questioning or flexing beyond the boundaries. Yet, within those rules and fences, an individual and a team could do whatever they thought best. In fact, most people felt secure and pretty happy. They knew the rules of the game, and they found ways to operate within them successfully without becoming Model I or defensive.

Make no mistake: defensive and learning organizations can show up in any of our four archetypes. There are also moments when Model I can serve the organization, such as during a crisis or when top-down directives are the only way to solve a problem. There are also moments when Model II can get in the way, such as having too much emphasis on consensus, difficulty making decisions, or even trouble with accountability. There is no perfect culture for all circumstances; that's why agility is so important.

My bias and my practice are to help organizations move from Model I to Model II by strengthening a culture's leadership competence in the four masteries, and then go beyond to Model III. I created Model III and call it the *aligned organization*. Model III takes the best from Models I and II and embeds *three powerful processes* within the larger system.

Model III: Aligned organizations foster attitudes and behaviors that:

- Align all stakeholders with the organization's mission, vision, and values.
- Are agile and adaptive and thus creative and resilient during change.
- Encourage reasonable risks—this culture encourages "failing forward."
- Demonstrate accountability for one's actions, behaviors, and business results in real time.
- Manage talent well—recruitment, hiring, training, performance management, and dignified separation—in line with the organization's mission, vision, values, and strategies.
- Plan for succession—growing a deep bench and developing others at all levels is an essential leadership responsibility and is measured.
- Measure and reward leaders for good business *and* good behavioral (values) results.

Consequences: learning and change lead to innovation, accountability is expected at all levels, and the culture is consistent and sustainable.

We need competence in the four masteries to move to Model II, and we need three processes in place to move to Model III (see Figure 22.2). Let's take a look at the definitions of the masteries and processes to see how they fit into the overall picture.

Figure 22.2   Moving from Model I to Model II to Model III

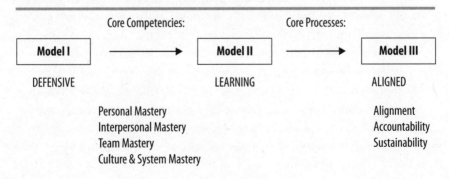

THE FOUR MASTERIES

- *Personal mastery.* This is the ability to know oneself and learn from experience. (Regular data, feedback loop, introspection, in learning mode, and risk taking.)
- *Interpersonal mastery.* This is the ability to communicate and work well with others, particularly in difficult and conflict-related situations. (Dialogue skills: listening, constructive feedback, and conflict.)
- *Team mastery.* This is the ability to develop and lead groups of individuals toward common goals while learning from experience. (Ground rules, shared mission, vision, values, utilizing the skills and motivation of all members, and effective leadership.)
- *Culture and systems mastery.* This is the ability to assess and consciously determine and create the desired culture. It includes the ability to think systemically and to lead the organization through a strategic change process in a way that develops commitment and learning. (Visioning, leading and managing change well, strategic planning, and effective and sustainable leadership.)

THE THREE PROCESSES

- *Alignment.* This is the purposeful alignment of business strategy with process, policy, and procedure in all core business activities. (Cradle-to-grave processes for organizational development and HR, financial and budget drivers, values and principles tied to business strategy.)
- *Accountability.* This is the critical link between expectations, measurement, and performance. It includes the fully integrated processes and connections that result in rewarding what the system wants and creating disincentives for what it does not want. (All incentives and rewards are tied to desired outcomes and are well known and communicated: hiring, training, promoting, and discipline.)
- *Sustainability.* This is the systematic and fully integrated growth and development of leaders, subject-matter experts (key individual contributors), and others both from within and from outside the organization in such a way that the desired culture and "bench strength" of

human capital are both sustained and grown purposefully. (Leaders are measured and rewarded for their effectiveness in growing others; systems are in place to track and manage talent.)

Many years ago, I came to understand how fragile Model II organizations are without these three core processes in place. For instance, Model II cultures have little ability to sustain their culture when a new leader arrives, fully loaded, with a very different culture in mind. Model III organizations, on the other hand, are not as leader-dependent. Their culture is deeply embedded in their DNA, meaning that it would take almost a complete transfusion of new blood to shift their commitment to their culture. This makes them far more sustainable and able to achieve better bottom-line results.

I've witnessed leaders who have failed, and failed fast, when they have tried to *whip this place* into their own image. No matter how hard they push against a strong, aligned culture, they won't win, unless, of course, they fire everyone and start over. That's akin to killing the patient, and then, at the very last minute, providing a shot of oxygen. I've seen that happen, too—and it ain't pretty!

In contrast, Model III aligned organizations can be so strong that a new leader has to pass deep systemic culture tests before even being hired. Either she will be a person who can help the culture and the organization grow stronger, or she will be spit out in no time.

Helen was the vice president of fundraising at a large university. She was a no-nonsense, take no prisoners, leader of a Model I organization, even though she ran a relationship and people business. She was amazingly successful with her alumni and board relationships, and therefore stayed in power. With her staff, she was unforgiving, showed favoritism, and wasn't interested in creating a Model II culture at all.

In order to eliminate 10 percent of her underperforming (in her mind) staff without having performance-related conversations; she simply terminated *everyone* and then required them all to reapply for the new jobs she created through restructuring. She hired back 90 percent of her people, some of them in new jobs and some in their old jobs. Everyone was shell-shocked, and many of her very best staff members were so appalled with her cutthroat approach, they left the minute they found other positions elsewhere.

(Continued)

The devastation from Helen's unilateral decision lasted far beyond her tenure. For at least 20 years, the stories about this incident have permeated the organization and have been passed on to new hires, sooner or later. A lot of healing had to be done. It is only in recent years, with Model II senior leadership in place, that the staff finally believes that it won't happen again.

Model III organizations tend to sustain themselves far longer than either Model I or Model II. They are also quite rare. For whatever reason, be it lack of tenure, skill, or will in the senior leadership, I have personally had only one client in all my years of practice, where senior leadership created a Model III culture and has successfully sustained it for several decades. Right here, right now I honor the Fanziska Racker Centers in upstate New York for a feat few have accomplished!

Other examples I am aware of are the "World Famous" Pike Place Fish Market in Seattle, which has been successfully maintaining its *fun* culture with people and fish for about 30 years. It inspired the "Fish Philosophy" of healthy, happy workplaces. Under Oprah Winfrey's leadership, her company culture is likely a Model III culture and has been for more than 30 years. It could be argued that the Zappos culture is so strong that when CEO Tony Hsieh leaves the company someday, it is likely to continue to thrive.

These are all good examples of Model III aligned, sustainable, accountable cultures that are deep and solid. While they are well known, they are still the standouts, not at all the cultural norm. I hope we can change that!

Most organizations don't get beyond Model II, and the descent to Model I can happen in the blink of an eye. You took the C.A.T. Scan to identify your predominant cultural archetype(s) or *cultural personality*. Now let's see which model is predominant in your team or organization.

Based on your own perceptions, take out your notebook to work on Exercise 39 and make a judgment call for each mastery and process. Then answer the questions at the end of the Exercise. For instance, if your culture has a good leadership training course that includes developing some or all of the four masteries in leaders and staff members, you might rank one or more of those masteries as Model II. You might place a Model III ranking under Accountability if your culture measures and then holds leaders accountable for practicing the leadership skills they learned. Knowing the skills only matters if you act on what you know.

Exercise 39
Where Is Your Team? (or Organization)

Write down I, II, or III for each mastery and process

- Personal mastery: _____   Model I, II, III
- Interpersonal mastery: _____   Model I, II, III
- Team mastery: _____   Model I, II, III
- Culture and Systems mastery: _____ Model I, II, III
- Alignment: _____   Model I, II, III
- Accountability: _____   Model I, II, III
- Sustainability: _____   Model I, II, III

1. Overall, is my team operating mostly in Model I, Model II, Model III, or somewhere in between?
2. Why do I think this?
3. What would my staff members say if I asked them these same questions?
4. Would the score be different for the larger organization as a whole?
5. Why do I think this?

A fair question to ask is, "How do I get to Model III?"

In the very beginning of this book, I said that I'd like you to put me out of business! This *is* the work I do for and with leaders and their organizations. People retain me to assess their culture and determine what needs to be done to create what they want it to be. I make recommendations and help the leaders get where they want to go, whether it's teaching or coaching the leaders how to lead a heck of a lot better; realigning their mission, vision, values, and strategies to meet their goals; helping them align their people systems; or building high-performing, high-functioning teams.

Most of those things I just listed you can do yourself. The simple truth is: you have to put your expectations in place and communicate them well, then *reward what you want and stop rewarding what you don't want.*

Whenever you make changes, you shake up your culture and your system one way or another. This happens even with small changes that may seem inconsequential to you. Never underestimate the ripple effect of a change decision!

Leading change well is a critical leadership skill within your system, so, of course, that's where we are headed in the next chapter.

Chapter 23

LEADING CHANGE

It is not the strongest of the species that survive, nor the most intelligent, but the one most responsive to change.
—CHARLES DARWIN

Whether the change at hand is large or small, or whether it's personal, about your team, or systemwide, the fundamentals of doing it well or doing it badly are the same. Making and leading change gracefully will help you achieve the results you want. Making and leading change badly will usually result in failure.

We are going to explore change in three ways. First, we will look at the realities of resistance to change, then we will consider the five common responses to change, and finally we will explore how you can lead change thoughtfully and successfully.

Change, even positive change, is often resisted when it is thrust upon people by the actions and decisions of others.

For Exercise 40, I'd like you to think of, and write down in your notebook, the answer to two questions.

Exercise 40
Two Change Questions

1. List three things (besides death and taxes) that *have not changed* in your life.
   a.   b.   c.

2. List three things that *have changed* in your life.
   a.   b.   c.

The answers to the "have not changed" question were probably harder to come up with than the "have changed" list. Is that right? Why is that?

Change is constant, the rate of change is accelerating, we work in an increasingly uncertain environment, we face escalating pressures to do more with less, and we believe that we must innovate or evaporate. Today, rapid change is *the new normal*. No matter whether it's a new tech toy or a new house or a new spouse, it seems that nothing stays the same, not even you. There is simply no escaping change, unless you choose to be a hermit in a cave, and even then, climate change will affect you!

We do need to find places to rest, or as I sometimes call them, places and spaces to *pause*, because constant upheaval and change, good or bad, wears us thin, burns us out, and lowers our resilience levels. I seriously encourage my clients to do this: take a *true break*, a real vacation, or at least stop taking on huge new projects for a couple of months. Let the dust settle. It's very important that you have time to think, observe, evaluate, regroup, and simply pause.

When you aren't on pause and you are initiating change, consider these *top 10* reasons why people resist change, in only slightly descending order of importance:

10. It caught me by surprise.
 9. I don't like leaving my "comfort zone."
 8. I don't understand the need for change.
 7. I understand the need, but I disagree with your solution.

6. I don't understand "what's in it for me."
5. I don't believe it will happen anyway.
4. I lack confidence and/or trust in the leaders.
3. I fear failure.
2. I fear loss.
1. I have no *voice* in the change that is affecting me.

Do you see anything in that list that sounds familiar? I have heard myself and other people say every one of those things at one time or another during a change process. It is not surprising that people often think and respond as Virginia Satir said, "The certainty of misery is better than the misery of uncertainty."

In addition, when change actually arrives, there are five very common and normal human responses that you can learn to navigate for yourself and when coaching and helping others. All of us have experienced these five responses at one time or another, sometimes in the space of a few minutes! They really are normal human responses. The trick is to feel them, deal with them, and then move out of four of them so that they don't debilitate you or others. Let's look at them one at a time.

FIVE RESPONSES TO CHANGE

The VICTIM

Behaviors. Resists change consistently, feels angry or depressed, thinks it's all about making him miserable, reverts to old ways of doing things.
Sounds like. Whine, whine, whine. "Why is this happening to *me*?" "Why can't things stay the same?" "What will *they* do to *me* this time?" "I hate that this always happens to me."
Get unstuck by. The victim response could be considered a shadow side of *Feeler* behavior. To get unstuck from this response, try to move toward *Thinker* behaviors, such as taking charge of and responsibility for what's happening in your life.

The CRITIC

Behaviors. Looks for reasons why change will *not* be a success; fails to see any positive outcomes from the change; thinks she knows better than everyone else.

Sounds like. "This has never worked before, and it won't work now." "*They* don't know what is going on or what they are doing!" "This will just make things worse." "This is stupid, and I can't wait to say, 'I told you so.'"

Get unstuck by. The critic response may be considered a shadow side of *Sensing* behavior. To get unstuck from this response, try to move toward *iNtuitive* behaviors, such as thinking about positive possibilities and opportunities that could occur because of the change. Consider how and what you could do to influence change.

Note: There is a difference between a critic and a resistor. Critics are naysayers without solutions or positive intent. Resistors come with ideas for alternative solutions and share their concerns based on positive intent. Resistors have important things to say for important reasons, whether they turn out to be right or wrong; listen to them.

The BYSTANDER

Behaviors. Acts reluctant to get involved; waits for others to take the lead; does not offer ideas.

Sounds like. "If I ignore this long enough, maybe it will go away." "I won't jump in until I know it's safe." "I'll wait until others have made the decisions."

Get unstuck by. The bystander response may be considered a shadow side of *iNtuitive* behavior. To get unstuck, try to move to *Sensing* behaviors, such as asking for more details and information; ask what role you might play in the change efforts, and don't withhold, but find ways to share your ideas.

The CHARGER

Behaviors. Leaps before looking; pushes others too hard—forces the issue; does not listen to other people and may even ignore new and important data.

Sounds like. "I know best, and I'll just force this to happen and be done with it!" "I don't need any more information." "Do it my way, and do it *now*!"

Get unstuck by. The charger response may be considered a shadow side of *Thinker* behavior. To get unstuck, try to move to *Feeler* behaviors such as considering how the change may affect others and trying to walk a mile in their shoes. Ask other people for input and engage them; listen to them carefully before making changes.

The NAVIGATOR

Behaviors. Looks for ways to reduce negative reactions; explores the reasons for the change and the impacts it will have; finds ways to be useful in the process; looks for opportunities to improve; forms positive and supportive relationships with those affected by the change.

Sounds like. "This change presents opportunities to do things differently." "It's a chance to do things better if we do it right." "I'm bound to make mistakes, but I'll learn from them." "I am in control of how I feel about and respond to the change." Being a navigator is a getting unstuck response. It is a balanced and centered attitude, and one that other people often respond to in positive ways. Being in this mode helps the person help herself and others move successfully through change. That can result in having more voice in and influence on the process.

It is not uncommon for a person to react to change by experiencing and expressing all five responses in a relatively short time. I've done it myself and I bet you have as well.

Frank, a senior vice president, decided to change every administrative computing system in our organization within just three years. Virtually every department and every person in the organization would feel the impact of these changes in huge ways. This was the right idea for change, but a disastrous execution of change. Along the way, Frank unilaterally decided that my division would be required to pay the lion's share of an entire retrofit of one of our internal systems so that it could link to his new central system. And by the way, it had to be done in four months, because he wasn't listening or caring when we told him this was a showstopper more than a year ago. Not only did we have to fix the problem we'd been warning about in record time, but we had to pay for his mistake.

I heard myself rant and rave through victim, critic, bystander, and charger, and finally land in the navigator response. And this all happened in the space of a one-hour meeting with my team! It was healthy because it was honest, I had empathy with their responses, and it was short. We all needed to vent, clear our heads, and then get down to business. In the end, we created the exact solution we needed, on time and under budget. We were proud of our work and the way we navigated a massive change that affected several thousand people.

Even small changes can evoke one or more of these responses from anyone. Remember, this is human, and it's normal. The key is to make sure that you don't linger too long in a negative place. Moving to navigator mode helps you and the people around you work through the changes. It also increases resilience during the change process. Being a navigator during stressful change demonstrates your Emotional Intelligence and increases trust in your leadership.

Directly or indirectly, our emotions affect our behaviors and actions; therefore, we need to pay attention to them. In your notebook, answer the questions in Exercise 41 about your own and others' responses to a recent change. Connect to the emotions around that change.

Exercise 41
Responses to Change

Think about a change you have recently experienced. *Be specific* with each question.

- What is the change?
- Who is involved in the change?
- What response(s) to this change have you noticed in yourself and others?
- What emotions did you feel or notice in others?
- How can YOU move into the NAVIGATOR response?
- What can you do to help others move into the NAVIGATOR response?

We now understand resistance and responses to change. The remaining question is, "How can you lead change well?" This is a *very* important question. You need to be able to lead change successfully without upsetting everyone who is touched by it.

For decades, significant research on the nature and reality of change within our organizations has told us the same story. It's a story that we need to really pay attention to. You may remember that Insight 7 in the first chapter of the book was, "Most change efforts fail." This is true in every sector of our society and any kind of enterprise. The biggest, "baddest," reasons that this is true are simple: most change efforts are top-down, and most of them are poorly conceived and/or poorly executed. Very few leaders even consider taking the time or making the effort to *map out their intended change process*—the why, who, what, where, when, and how—to ensure that they have covered the most important bases.

I'm not telling you anything you don't already know. Everywhere you look, in every sector of the work world, successful execution and integration of change initiatives is nothing short of ghastly. You've lived through them and suffered through them, and now you would like to prevent this from happening on your watch. Right? I sure hope so!

There is a better way. I've done it many times, I've helped other people do it, and I've witnessed the positive results when change efforts are executed well. A great place to start is to turn upside down the way most people initiate change. *Instead of pushing change on people, pull it.* I call this "Filling Your Bucket" with the bottomless well of wisdom found in the minds and hearts of your people. Do this well, and you will see your influence and others' trust in you grow! Start by answering the questions in Exercise 42.

Exercise 42
Change Result Questions

1. Consider memorable changes that you have experienced at work (or at home) that have gone *well*. Make a list of reasons why.
2. Consider memorable changes that you have experienced at work (or at home) that have gone *badly*. Make a list of reasons why.
3. What conclusions can you draw from your answers?

All change processes that work have at least *eight characteristics in common*. Let's run one fairly complex change through these eight characteristics to see how they play out. This is a *real* case study of a successful change initiative.

1. *Develop a shared vision of the end state and enroll stakeholders in the vision.* The change initiative did not begin well. The vision was imposed by senior management. Within one year, the division was required to reduce the number of financial professionals by two full-time equivalents (FTEs) and centralize all decentralized business office functions to serve numerous departments. Upon receiving this edict, an internal vision was created and shared:
   - To make these changes with the least amount of pain and disruption to people and work
   - As a result of the change, to create opportunities for staff members and efficiencies for departments
2. *Involve the key stakeholders and build consensus around the need for change.* Everyone who was affected, from support staff to department heads, was engaged in meetings and focus groups. Some were interviewed; some worked on the core team in off-site retreats; some

attended full staff meetings. A core change team with an executive sponsor to support it was created to guide the process.

3. *Identify and share explicitly the change model and process you will be using.* The core change team developed a model. It mapped out the change process with milestones and timelines, along with roles, responsibilities, and accountabilities.

4. *Develop the plan: what, how, who, when?* All these questions were answered within the change model. If and when changes had to be made along the way, those who were affected were involved and informed.

5. *Get Started! Identify some quick wins.* One FTE to cut was identified immediately: there was an unfilled vacancy, and this could be counted. Still, the goal was to meet or beat the budget. The core change team was delighted to tell everyone that they had to find only one more FTE within the fiscal year. Management had promised to avoid any layoffs, making an explicit commitment to either find the FTE by voluntary attrition or to support anyone who wanted to seek a different role outside the finance group. In addition, the affected staff team was asked to suggest multiple options for redesigning roles and job duties to best serve the soon to be centralized finance functions for the departments and the division by utilizing the skill sets that they already had and identifying any skill sets that were missing.

6. *Monitor and refine the process.* There were regular check-ins with the stakeholders. There were a few rough moments when gossip got out of hand and communication was less than rigorous. The solution was to catch the problem quickly, name it, own it, clean it up, and ensure better communications methods going forward.

7. *Embed the new realities organizationally.* Once staff recommendations were reviewed and discussed, and some modifications were made and agreed to, the changes were implemented. One person accepted, with some pain, a lower-paying position, and another person found a different role within the division that was a better fit for his skill set. Every department customer had access to more resources than before because the staff members were cross-trained.

8. *Celebrate! Provide support for new and desired behaviors.* Once the changes were agreed to, there was a celebration. Once the changes were implemented, there was another, larger celebration to honor

the top-notch collaborative effort and the success of the project. The team beat both the budget and the time requirements, coming in way ahead of schedule and being the first division in the organization to complete. Nearly everyone was excited about the new opportunities for learning and growth that had opened up. The departments, which had been highly skeptical and resistant to losing control over their "people," were relieved at the relative lack of disruption and the efficiencies that resulted. While the change process wasn't without any pain or without any glitches, it was a clear success.

All successful changes have the same key components. A change process is simply a *map* for a very specific trip that you plan to make. That map needs to make sense both to you and to anyone who is going on that particular trip with you. It needs to guide your organization along the way with well-understood and well-defined checkpoints and stopovers.

When I boil down all my experiences with successful change, I end up with these three things:

1. *Engage* all the people affected by the change in the vision, design, planning, implementation, and evaluation of the changes.
2. *Empower* all the people affected by the change to take risks, innovate, and take action.
3. *Embed* what works within your systems, processes, and policies, and eliminate what doesn't work.

In every change process, there are predictable things that happen. You will need to "unfreeze," the current state, then change to a new state, and finally "refreeze" to the desired new state.

I am providing you with three different *change models* to help you navigate the *change process* well. You can use them as is, mix and match, or draw from them to build your own. They all have vision, engagement, communication, and integration in common. The eight characteristics that I listed in the case study are found within these models. Engage, empower, and embed is simply shorthand for the all steps in these models. So take a look; see what resonates with you.

At the end of the day, it doesn't matter what model you use. *It matters that you use a model and have a process,* and that you communicate it clearly to all those who are affected by the change!

THE KOTTER MODEL[1]

1. Establishing a sense of urgency:
   a. Examining market and competitive realities
   b. Identifying and discussing crises, potential crises, and opportunities

2. Forming a powerful guiding coalition:
   a. Assembling a group with enough power to lead the change effort
   b. Encouraging the group to work together as a team

3. Creating a vision:
   a. Creating a vision to help direct the change effort
   b. Developing strategies to achieve that vision

4. Communicating the vision:
   a. Using every vehicle possible to communicate the vision and strategies
   b. Teaching the new behaviors by the example of the guiding coalition

5. Empowering others to act on the vision:
   a. Getting rid of obstacles to change
   b. Changing systems and structures that seriously undermine the vision
   c. Encouraging risk taking and nontraditional ideas, activities, and actions

6. Planning for and creating short-term wins:
   a. Planning for visible performance improvements
   b. Creating those improvements
   c. Recognizing and rewarding employees involved in improvements

7. Consolidating improvements and producing more change:
   a. Using increased credibility to change systems and policies that don't fit
   b. Hiring, promoting, and developing employees who can support the vision
   c. Reinvigorating the process with new projects and change agents

8. Institutionalizing new approaches:
   a. Articulating the connections between new behaviors and corporate success
   b. Developing the means to ensure leadership development and succession

THE GE MODEL[2]

SUCCESS FACTORS	KEY QUESTIONS
Leading change (Who is responsible?)	Do we have a leader . . . Who owns and champions the change? Who publicly commits to making it happen? Who will garner the resources to sustain it? Who will put in the time to follow through?
Creating a shared need (Why do it?)	Do employees . . . See the reason for the change? Understand why it is important? See how it will help them in the short and long term?
Shaping a vision (What will it look like when we're done?)	Do employees . . . See the outcomes of the change in terms of what they will do differently? Get excited about the results of the change? Understand how it will benefit stakeholders?
Mobilizing commitment (Who else needs to be involved?)	Do the sponsors of the change . . . Recognize who else needs to be committed? Know how to build a coalition of support? Have the ability to enlist key individuals? Have the ability to build a responsibility matrix?
Modifying systems and structures (How will the change be integrated?)	Do sponsors of the change . . . Understand how to link it to other systems, such as staffing, training, appraisal, rewards, structure, and communications? Recognize the systems implications?
Monitoring progress (How will the change be measured?)	Do the sponsors of the change . . . Have a means of measuring its success? Plan to benchmark progress against both results and the process of implementation?
Making it last (How will it get started and last?)	Do the sponsors of the change . . . Recognize the first steps in getting started? Have a short- and long-term plan to keep attention focused on the change? Have a plan to adapt the change over time?

Figure 23.1   Company X Change Management Process

FOUNDATION	PROCESS	LAUNCH	LOGISTICS	INTEGRATE
Strategy	Design	Create	Act	Assess
Vision	Process Plan	Teams in Motion	Build Stakeholder Relationships	Continuity Plan
Purpose	People Plan	Monitor Progress	Training	Evaluation
Impact Analysis	Resource Plan		Support	Integrate Learning
	Communication Plan		Continuity plan	New Normal
GO? No GO?	GO? No GO?	GO? No GO?		END

Milestones ▲	▲	▲	▲
Communication	Measurement	Communication	Measurement	Communication

Here's the good news. People tend to embrace change faster when:

- They understand the need for change as well as the change process.
- They are truly heard and involved.
- They trust the change leader.
- They understand the negative consequences of not changing.
- The perceived gains exceed the perceived losses.
- Their peers adopt the change.

Here are some commonsense considerations:

- Prevent and avoid surprises.
- Be honest and transparent about what you can and cannot share.
- Involve those who are in any way affected by the change.
- Be patient and persistent.
- Ask for and listen to the voices of your people every single step of the way.
- Communicate, communicate, communicate!

No doubt you picked up the resounding theme in all this: *people*. If you do not get buy-in, you will get dropouts. It is the *people* who make or break any change effort, no matter how much sense the change makes to you and no matter how clever you've mapped it out. Getting your people on board with the change is the only way it can be sustainable. This is the primary failing of most change efforts; the right people are not in the equation in the right way at the right time—from start to finish.

Yes, we all know that change is not going to stop, go away, or even decrease. But let's not complain too much about that. The stagnation and atrophy train is not a better ride. We all want the best changes to happen in the best ways. We also want the results to be positive. This means that we need to become competent and confident when we are leading change. It also means that we need to have the patience to make a plan and then work the plan so that the changes stick. And if they don't stick, it was all a gross waste of everyone's time and resources.

There is a lot of terrific information out there in the world that delves deeply into managing change. And...if you *only* do what I've suggested here, you will do very well.

With shared accountability to and for a change process, good things happen. It so happens that the next chapter is all about accountability, a topic that hits hot buttons for a lot of people.

Chapter 24

ACCOUNTABILITY

There is no such thing as a minor lapse in integrity.
—TOM PETERS

Definition: Accountability is our promise. It means that we take ownership of and responsibility for the outcomes of our choices.

Those choices speak directly to our integrity and our trustworthiness. Accountability is a mirror that reflects our character. When we are leaders, we must accept accountability for our actions and behaviors. We also have a responsibility to ensure that those whom we lead are accountable for their actions and behaviors.

Here is a simple model to help us understand this dynamic. There are only three factors to consider:

1. *Expectations and learning.* Everyone needs to know exactly what is expected of him or her to succeed. That includes any additional or new learning needed to meet behavior, task, and result expectations.
2. *Measurement and feedback.* Everyone needs to know exactly how performance will be measured. People need to understand exactly how and when they will receive feedback.

3. *Acknowledgement of performance.* Everyone should know what will happen if performance results meet or exceed expectations and what will happen if they don't.

Figure 24.1   Accountability Model

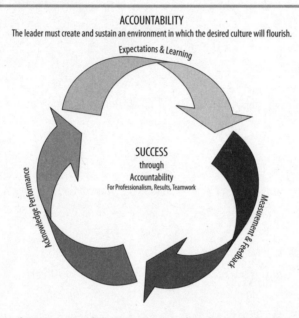

This is a dynamic model; at any time there may be new information, changes in priorities, or other factors that may create a need to recalibrate expectations or metrics. When this happens, the leader and/or the employee need to revisit the cycle and redefine what success looks like now.

Marcus was a bright, hardworking staff member who was failing miserably at his job. He couldn't meet his metrics, and I kept having to give him bad news when discussing his performance. In our regular expectations and learning discussion, he finally told me that he really wanted to do a very different job, something that he loved doing and would even volunteer to do whenever he had the chance. After a lot of exploring and brainstorming, I assigned him on an interim basis to a job that fit his needs and expectations while meeting my business needs. Marcus took it upon himself to learn what he needed to learn for the new role, and his performance soared. He was permanently assigned to the job and even got a bonus a year later. I learned a lot from that experience. I learned to listen carefully to my staff members' expectations and to look harder for the root causes of performance problems.

I'd like you to think about one person in your life—at work or at home—whose behaviors and/or actions aren't matching up with your expectations. You might want to use your notebook to jot down your answers. Let's take a walk around the accountability circle and ask yourself the questions in Exercises 43a and 43b.

Exercise 43a
Accountability Reality Check

1. Have we had explicit conversations about what I expect and what this person expects? If so, was any new learning required to be successful?

2. Have we talked about how we would measure these expectations?

3. Have I given this person clear, constructive feedback about those results?

4. In what ways have I acknowledged this person's performance?

5. Have I acknowledged performance (good or bad) with or without talking about the other two steps? Be specific if yes or no is the answer.

The second half of this exercise is about *you* and your own accountability.

Exercise 43b
Accountability Reality Check

1. Are there any places in your life where you haven't kept your promises to someone else?

2. If there are, check the accountability model: Are the expectations of you clear? Do you know what success looks like? Do you receive constructive feedback? Are there any positive or negative consequences when you do or do not keep your promises?

I'm sure you get the idea—and that means that you are ready to use the model in all parts of your life if you choose to do so. You now have a solid accountability model that anyone can understand. It is simple and easy to use. You can add your own explanations to it. Some of my clients have adapted it to their language and culture with great success. The success of our teams and our organizations depends on everyone taking responsibility for holding each other and ourselves accountable when it comes to our promises. That's trust, and that's integrity.

A topic that is both close to my heart and close to accountability is recognition. Let's take a good look at that in the next chapter.

Chapter 25

RECOGNITION

*There are two things people want more than sex
or money . . . recognition and praise.*
—MARY KAY ASH

Definition: Recognition is the simple act of acknowledging, approving, or appreciating a behavior or an action.

Anytime you treat someone like a worthwhile human being, this can be considered recognition. You can give recognition to a staff member, a supervisor, a colleague, a customer, a family member, a friend, or even a stranger on the street.

In my experience, people often fall into the trap of focusing on what is not working rather than on what is working, whether it concerns themselves, their lives, or their relationships with other people. I understand that trap, and I urge you to stay out of it. Life is either half full or half empty; you get to decide, and your entire life and your relationships will reflect that decision.

People everywhere respond far more readily to appreciation, positive reinforcement, or even what you'd like them to start doing, than they do to negative reinforcement, punishment, or what you want them to stop doing. Of course, your appreciation has to be genuine, specific, and timely. I encourage you to do this when it is deserved, and do it often.

I once worked with a shop supervisor whose staff morale was very low. He proudly told me that he never thanked anyone. He said, and I quote, "They get a paycheck every two weeks. That should be thanks enough!" I told him that if that was all the thanks his staff members ever heard from him, all he would get from them would be the minimum effort they could get away with for that paycheck, and never anything above and beyond. That concept had never occurred to him.

Please write down the answers to the two questions about recognition in Exercise 44.

Exercise 44
Recognition Reality Check

1. When was the last time someone *genuinely thanked* you in some way for something? What was it for? What did the person say?
   - How did each of those interactions feel to you?
   - How much time did it take?
   - What did it cost?
2. When was the last time you *genuinely thanked* someone for something? What was it for? What did you say?
   - How did each of those interactions feel to you?
   - How did that person respond?
   - How much time did it take?
   - What did it cost?

When I said *genuinely thanked*, I meant more than a simple "thank you," although those also matter. My intent was more along constructive feedback lines for positive reinforcement of behaviors or actions that are appreciated. It's the difference between, "Hey, thanks for picking up my kids today," and, "I am so grateful to you for taking the time and going out of your way to pick my kids up from practice. It made such a difference to me to be able to finish that project at work. Thank you!" Do you see the difference? One is a nice "by the way," while the other is heartfelt, explicit, and meaningful.

Six Recognition Facts

1. Recognition builds trust.
2. Recognition is an investment in your most valuable resource (people), and it improves performance.
3. People require appreciation in order to be happy in their jobs.
4. Recognition carries more cachet when it comes from the leader, *and* it is everyone's responsibility to recognize positive behaviors and actions.
5. One size does not fit all; different things motivate people at different times.
6. Managers think they give recognition 90 percent of the time, but staff members think they get it only 10 percent of the time. People who have never received it often don't know how to give it.

Six Barriers to Giving Recognition (Myths)

People often believe the following myths:

1. It takes too much time.
2. It costs money.
3. It will make staff members "soft."
4. It's appropriate only for superstars and highly extraordinary results.
5. It's understood by everyone and doesn't need to be openly stated.
6. It's favoritism if everyone doesn't receive the same or equal recognition.

All expressions of recognition are appreciated when they are genuine. It is an integral part of any healthy, happy culture.

As you begin to consider how to recognize others, give your plan my *"MATS"* test. Ask yourself, is it: Meaningful to the receiver(s), Authentic, Timely, and Specific?

What's in it for you? A lot! Did you know that expressing gratitude regularly can increase your own happiness and make you physically healthier? It's true. It can actually affect your body's functions in many remarkable ways. You could begin to see increases in optimism, determination, attention, enthusiasm, and energy, along with a reduction in physical ailments. All this with no pills![1]

There are many low- and no-cost ideas for showing your gratitude and recognizing others. I'd like you to think up as many as you can. In your notebook, make a list of your ideas. Keep a clean page open for new ideas as they occur to you or as you read about them.

Exercise 45
List of Low- and No-Cost Recognition Ideas

1. I can say "thank you" to someone every single day with specifics and meaning.
2.
3.
4.
5. Keep your list going . . .

It's time to ask yourself, "How can I increase my expression of gratitude by recognizing others in my work and my home life?" Make a plan to do exactly that, today, tomorrow, and all the tomorrows to come. It will change your life in remarkable ways.

In the next chapter, we're going to delve into the topic of leadership courage—in yourself, your teams, and your entire organization. It's not for the faint of heart! You will see a model that will help you actually measure your courage and help you to make decisions going forward.

Chapter 26

COURAGE

You gain strength, courage, and confidence by every experience in which you really stop to look fear in the face. You must do the thing which you think you cannot do.
—ELEANOR ROOSEVELT

What is courage? In *The Wizard of Oz*, the Lion was seeking courage, unaware that he had it inside himself all along. In this chapter, we are going to define courage, understand the role it plays in leadership, and learn how to measure it from four different perspectives. There are many, many definitions of courage; they have a great deal in common, and I offer this one.

Definition: Courage is the quality of the mind or spirit that enables us to face physical or moral difficulty, danger, pain, and other hardships and walk toward and through them anyway.

Courage can mean different things to different people at different times. I'd like you to think about and write down in your notebook, the answer to the question in Exercise 46.

Exercise 46
What Does Courage Mean to You?

What are three words or statements that exemplify courage to you?

1.
2.
3.

We are going to explore the topic of courage by using the MBTI functions of Sensing, iNtuition, Thinking, and Feeling one more time. You'll see why it makes sense to do so as we go through each, one by one.

Jamie was working for a Model I organization that was pretending to be a Model II. It was one of those almost cultlike cultures where people and values were supposed to be honored by everyone, but she soon saw that the reality was much more sinister. The truth was, the values were only window dressing and were manipulated to suit the leaders' agendas. Their actions were anything but aligned with their stated values. When Jamie realized this and refused a direct order to do something that she knew was unethical, she was severely reprimanded by her supervisors. Rather than continue to try to lead her people in a fake culture where the actual values were in direct opposition to hers, for the first time in her life, she quit without first finding another job. Her courage paid off. She found another job that suited her almost immediately, her health improved, and the former company's top leaders all disappeared when another company acquired them.

If you recall, Sensing and iNtuition are the ways in which we make sense of our world. Thinking and Feeling are the ways in which we prefer to make decisions. These will help us understand the courage we can tap into and the challenges we may need to overcome. When we look at courage from these four perspectives, something fascinating begins to emerge.

Sensors often have the courage to question other people's assumptions because they pay attention to facts and details. Their courage challenge is to try something they've never tried before because they are less comfortable with change and risk than they are with the current state.

iNtuitives often have the courage to embrace change because of their big-picture perspective and their fascination with possibilities. Their courage challenge is to accept rigor and stick with something to the finish because they would prefer to go on to the next idea rather than focus on the details of the current one.

Thinkers often demonstrate the courage to do whatever it takes to accomplish their goal because of their motivation for achievement. Their courage challenge is to express empathy and to understand their own and others' emotions.

Feelers often demonstrate the courage to do what is right for people no matter what because of their commitment to relationships and fairness. Their courage challenge is to make tough decisions even when they may be unpopular or cause disharmony.

I've created a questionnaire for you called the Courage Quotient, or CQ. You can record your answers on the CQ Map Grid that I've provided. Once you map your answers, you will have a good idea of your (or your team's) particular strengths and weaknesses when it comes to courage. These questions can also be used for families and for entire organizations.

Exercise 47
The Courage Quotient (CQ)

Circle any statement where you can answer a ***strong yes***. Map your answers on the CQ Map Grid. When using for a team, replace "I" with "We."

Thinking: The Courage to Tell It Like It Is and Get It Done

1. I name and address difficult topics or touchy subjects openly and with candor.
2. I disagree respectfully and without assuming an adversarial stance.
3. I have the willingness to shift my priorities when the data or the needs of others indicate a need for change.
4. I have a "can do" attitude.
5. I use decision-making protocols that make it clear who has what authority.
6. I take pride in the results of joint efforts as well as my own.

(Continued)

Feeling: The Courage to Do the Right Thing for People

7. I run meetings so that everyone has an opportunity to contribute.
8. I use humor appropriately in groups.
9. I respect differences in roles, backgrounds, perspectives and the like, within the group.
10. I address conflicts and attitudinal, behavioral, or performance issues that could affect others and the work results.
11. I help promote a culture of trust and "assume the best first" within groups.
12. I set aside my personal agenda and priorities when doing so results in positive outcomes for the greater good.

Sensing: The Courage to Ask the Hard Questions

13. I take risks that expose me to potential failure in order to achieve an important goal.
14. I use a well-conceived process so that the necessary facts, possibilities, and consequences are considered and vetted before decisions are made.
15. I establish and utilize methods to ensure high standards.
16. I ensure that necessary information and resources are readily available.
17. I learn from my experiences, then apply my learning and share it with others.
18. I keep my promises, follow through, and hold myself accountable.

Intuition: The Courage to Envision a New and Better Future

19. I have a high level of alignment among the big-picture vision, organizational strategies, and my role.
20. I imagine and then reach for stretch goals that are outside of my comfort zone.
21. I apply focus and structure to my creative thinking processes.
22. I have enthusiasm for my role and the challenges I face.
23. I adapt well to changes, unexpected setbacks, or even failures when they occur.
24. I demonstrate an attitude of optimism toward others and the work we are doing.

Transfer Your Answers to the CQ Map Grid

Note: For a team CQ, change the "I" in each question to "We."
CQ Map Grid
Directions: Place a "√" in the boxes for the questions you answered with a strong *yes*.

Thinking	Feeling	Sensing	Intuition
1.	7.	13.	19.
2.	8.	14.	20.
3.	9.	15.	21.
4.	10.	16.	22.
5.	11.	17.	23.
6.	12.	18.	24.

Add the total number of √s for each of the four factors.

Thinking	Feeling	Sensing	Intuition

Map your total scores to the following chart by placing a dot on the broken horizontal line that corresponds to the total score for each factor. Connect the dots to create a graph of your own or your team's current level of courage.

6 —	6 —	6 —	6 —
5 —	5 —	5 —	5 —
4 —	4 —	4 —	4 —
3 —	3 —	3 —	3 —
2 —	2 —	2 —	2 —
1 —	1 —	1 —	1 —
Thinking	**Feeling**	**Sensing**	**Intuition**

What now?

Naturally, any score of 5 or 6 is a good one. Any score of 4 or less is something that you may want to pay attention to. Look for patterns that validate or challenge your own perceptions. Taken individually, the 24 questions provide excellent specific material for discussion and planning your next steps.

Those columns with the most and least questions checked will likely indicate where your courage is strongest and where it may need improvement. Once you complete this exercise, consider what work needs to be done to *boost* the lower courage scores and continue to *enhance* the high courage scores.

You can map various teams to see what the differences among them are. You can also ask individual team members to answer the questions to assess how consistent or inconsistent their perceptions are. You can also do this with multiple stakeholders to take a perception snapshot of the organization. All of this will tell you a story.

Here are some indicators to consider:

High Thinking scores indicate that you are not caught up in just "getting it done," but you also have the Emotional Intelligence and wisdom to know that candid yet positive interpersonal relationships are critical factors in getting it done.

Low Thinking scores may mean that you can get stuck in the "winning the race" mindset and forget the people who will or won't help you get you there.

High Feeling scores indicate that you generally take all people into account while still holding them accountable for their behaviors and results.

Low Feeling scores may mean that you have work to do to engage the team members in a trusting manner with the greater good kept in mind, and to learn to deal with conflicts and accountability in a timely and appropriate manner.

High Sensing scores indicate you are willing to take reasonable risks while looking at the bigger picture that includes facts, possibilities, and potential consequences. Accountability is important to you.

Low Sensing scores may mean that you may be too concerned about making a mistake and taking risks rather than getting the job done, and you could both get stuck in the minutiae and find yourself ignoring the people around you.

High iNtuitive scores indicate that you can both imagine and focus on your work to achieve your goals. You are likely to be positive, agile, and reasonably comfortable with risk taking.

Low iNtuitive scores may mean that you are having difficulty with seeing the big picture and with taking risks. You may be too critical of yourself and others, leading to a lack of openness to learning and new ideas.

Courage Final Thoughts

- We know courage when we feel it and see it in ourselves and others.
- Any time you step out of your comfort zone into a place of learning and risk, you are exhibiting courage.
- Courage doesn't require an act of heroism. It is an act of courage to say, "I choose to try something new or to take a risk."

Consider the journey we've taken together throughout this book, and now consider what we've just explored about courage. You've done a lot of work if you've completed all the exercises. At the end of the day, it takes courage to:

- Look closely at yourself.
- Admit what you don't know about leadership.
- Learn and apply the skills that will make you a better leader of people.
- Stand up for your values.
- Admit your mistakes and be vulnerable.
- Lead successful change and be accountable for the results.
- Decide you could be better at your relationships and choose to improve them.
- Lead people where they may not know they need to go.

Key Learnings for Culture
and Systems Mastery

1. Culture is "the way we do things here," and the leader's number one job is to create and nurture the culture that she wants and expects in the workplace over which she has responsibility.
2. The four cultural archetypes are the four Ps: People, Possibility, Product, and Policy. We can measure our "cultural personality" by using the C.A.T. Scan (Cultural Analysis Tool).
3. Moving from Model I to Model II requires the four masteries. Moving to Model III requires adding the three core processes of alignment, accountability, and sustainability.
4. The five responses to change are victim, critic, bystander, charger, and navigator.
5. The number one reason that people resist change is that they believe or feel that they have *no voice* in the decisions that are affecting them.
6. When you *engage* your people, *empower* them to have a voice in decisions, and *embed* the changes in the fabric of your organization, you will have a good shot at "buy-in," and that means that the change is likely to stick.
7. Choose a change process, and communicate it to everyone who will be affected, and then *pull* rather than *push* change in your organization.
8. Accountability in the system comes about when each person knows *explicitly* what is expected of him, how his work will be measured, and how and when his performance will be acknowledged.
9. Use the "MATS" test to make sure that recognition matches the situation and the person.
10. Courage is the quality of the mind or spirit that enables us to face physical or moral difficulty, danger, pain, and other hardships and walk toward and through them anyway.

Chapter 27

SUMMING UP

A journey of a thousand miles begins with a single step.
—LAO-TZU

What a journey we've had together!

Let's take a walk down memory lane and figuratively flip through the pages of this book.

We began with the *eight insights* and came to understand why we need to "lead like it matters." We moved on to *personal mastery*, understanding your own preferences and style, learning about building your Emotional Intelligence competencies, and being grounded in your own values, purpose, and vision.

Then we tackled *interpersonal mastery*. Becoming adept at the dialogue skills of deep listening, constructive feedback, and conflict management will give you the confidence to have the conversations that you need to have. We learned how increasing your interpersonal mastery skills will build trust in you as a person and as a leader.

In *team mastery*, we discovered how important it is to have everyone working together in the same direction. We walked up the *pay now or pay later* stepladder model for teams with a shared purpose who need to build safety, trust, and group identity in order to achieve your goals and decide on your future vision. We found that having a shared vision, mission, and values will get you where you want to go much faster, better, and cheaper— a bit like being turbocharged.

Along the way, many decisions have to be made. Now you know the questions to ask and have the tools to make good decisions. We learned that delegation, well done, is a powerful win/win way to develop your people and liberate yourself.

We paused along our path to explore bad and good meetings. We know how to compute the cost of a meeting. We can consciously create meetings that are a worthwhile expenditure of time and money by using effective meeting tools.

You know that the trust others have in you begins with you. You know that you can succeed with your work, your teams, and throughout your organization only when you can trust and be trusted. Trust = Success!

And finally, after a nice long walk through *culture and systems mastery*, you know that your culture is all around you and that, as a leader, you are responsible for what happens within your sphere of influence, or your "pond." To help you do that, we went through a lot of material on cultural archetypes and models and assessed your culture through the C.A.T. Scan.

We then explored resistance and responses to change and how you can navigate and lead change so that you and your team can be agile and adapt to new realities as they arise.

We reinforced the notion that holding ourselves and others accountable for behaviors and actions that are in harmony with our values *and* business results is going to make or break us. Recognizing one another becomes part of the acknowledgment that we are in this together.

And finally, we pulled it all together into a neat package when we took a big toe-dip into the notion of courage. We can safely say that courage does not require an act of physical or even extraordinary heroism. It is an act of courage to simply say, "I choose to take a risk out of my comfort zone, and to learn." We know courage in ourselves and in others when we feel it and see it.

I applaud you for investing in yourself and your career, and I thank you for trusting me to travel on this journey with you. You can reinforce your learning by reading the chapters again and repeating the exercises that resonated with you. You can also choose to take the companion online course at www.askroxi.com using your special book coupon code *askroxileader* to cut the price in half.

To continue on this journey, it will help you to share with others what you've learned, and create a safe and courageous environment where your people can do their best work.

All I hope for is that, from this day forward, you consciously choose to:

Lead like It Matters . . . Because It Does!

Notes

INTRODUCTION

1. Mark Busine, Bruce Watt, Richard S. Wellins, and Jazmine Boatman, "Driving Workplace Performance Through High-Quality Conversations: What Leaders Must Do Every Day to Be Effective," Development Dimensions International; 2013; https://www.ddiworld.com/productivity/overview.
2. Susan Adams, "New Survey: Majority of Employees Dissatisfied," *Forbes*, May 18, 2012; http://www.forbes.com/sites/susanadams/2012/05/18/new-survey-majority-of-employees-dissatisfied/.
3. Gallup, "State of the American Workplace: Employee Engagement Insights for U.S. Business Leaders," 2013; http://www.gallup.com/strategicconsulting/163007/state-american-workplace.aspx.
4. Beth Stebner, "Workplace Morale Heads Down: 70% of Americans Negative About Their Jobs, Gallup Study Shows," *New York Daily News*, June 24, 2013; http://www.nydailynews.com/news/national/70-u-s-workers-hate-job-poll-article-1.1381297#ixzz2sxCLpeTh.
5. Keith Grant, "Americans Hate Their Jobs and Even Perks Don't Help," *Today*, Money, June 24, 2013; http://www.today.com/money/americans-hate-their-jobs-even-perks-dont-help-6C10423977.

CHAPTER 1

1. Brent Ruben, *Pursuing Excellence in Higher Education: Eight Fundamental Challenges* (San Francisco: Jossey-Bass, 2003), pp. 288–314.
2. For a discussion of the Pareto principle, see http://management.about.com/cs/generalmanagement/a/Pareto081202.htm and http://en.wikipedia.org/wiki/Pareto_principle.
3. M. Beer and N. Nohria, "Cracking the Code of Change," *Harvard Business Review* 78, no. 3 (2000): 133–141.
4. J. P. Kotter, *A Sense of Urgency* (Boston: Harvard Business School Press, 2008).

243

CHAPTER 2

1. Peter M. Senge, *The Fifth Discipline* (New York: Doubleday, 1990, p. 7).

CHAPTER 3

1. Source: Emotional and Social Competency Inventory (ESCI). © 2014 Daniel Goleman, Richard Boyatzis and Hay Group. Emotional Intelligence: All references to Emotional Intelligence are drawn from the Emotional Intelligence Training Materials supplied to Certified EI Professionals by the Hay Group and are based on the work of Daniel Goleman, PhD, and Richard Boyatzis, PhD. Roxana B. Hewertson is a Hay Group Certified EI Practitioner.
2. Daniel Goleman, *Emotional Intelligence* (New York: Bantam Books–Doubleday, 1995).
3. Daniel Goleman, Richard Boyatzis, and Annie McKee, *Primal Leadership* (Boston: Harvard Business School Press, 2002).

CHAPTER 5

1. Life Line: with permission from Rodney Napier, The Napier Group, Pottstown, PA.

CHAPTER 6

1. Milton Rokeach, *The Nature of Human Values* (New York: Free Press, 1973).

CHAPTER 7

1. Ken Blanchard et al., *Leading at a Higher Level* (Harlow, NJ: Financial Times Press, 2007). Susan Fowler developed this process for the Situational Self Leadership program offered by the Ken Blanchard Companies. For more information, go to http://www.kenblanchard.com.

CHAPTER 8

1. Natalie Goldberg, *Writing Down the Bones* (Boston: Shambhala Publications, 2005).
2. Robert Gass, "The Art of Leadership," course at the Omega Institute Workshops, Rhinebeck, NY, 2008.
3. Ibid.

CHAPTER 9

1. Susan Scott, *Fierce Conversations* (New York: Berkley Books, 2002, 2004).
2. Ibid.
3. Chris Argyris and Donald A. Schön, *Organizational Learning II: Theory, Method, and Practice* (Reading, MA: Addison-Wesley, 1996).

CHAPTER 11

1. Ken Blanchard and Spencer Johnson, *The One Minute Manager* (New York: William Morrow & Co. 1982).

CHAPTER 12

1. Michael Feiner, *The Feiner Points of Leadership* (New York: Warner Business Books, 2004).
2. Michael Useem, *Leading Up* (New York: Three Rivers Press, 2001).

CHAPTER 13

1. Chris Argyris, *Overcoming Organizational Defenses* (Englewood Cliffs, NJ: Prentice-Hall, 1990).

CHAPTER 14

1. Jon Katzenbach and Douglas Smith, *The Wisdom of Teams*, (New York: HarperCollins, 1994, 1999).

CHAPTER 15

1. Bruce Tuckman, "Developmental Sequence in Small Groups," *Psychological Bulletin* 63, no. 6 (1965): 384–399; and http://www.businessballs.com/tuckman formingstormingnormingperforming.htm.
2. For more information on Maslow's hierarchy of needs, see http://www.simply psychology.org/maslow.html.

CHAPTER 18

1. http://www.nwlink.com/~donclark/hrd/media/70-20-10.html
2. Paul Hersey and Ken H. Blanchard, "Life cycle theory of leadership," *Training and Development Journal*, 1969, 23 (5), 26–34.

CHAPTER 19

1. Thomas Kayser, *Mining Group Gold* (New York: McGraw-Hill, 2010).

CHAPTER 20

1. Paul Hersey and Ken H. Blanchard, "Life Cycle Theory of Leadership," *Training and Development Journal* 23, no. 5 (1969): 26–34.
2. Dov Seidman, "Building Trust in Business by Trusting," *Bloomberg Businessweek*, August 27, 2009; http://www.businessweek.com/magazine/content/09_36/ b4145076753447.htm.

CHAPTER 21

1. James S. Kunen, "Enron's Vision (and Values) Thing," *New York Times*, January 19, 2002; http://www.nytimes.com/2002/01/19/opinion/enron-s-vision-and-values-thing.html.

CHAPTER 22

1. Chris Argyris, *Overcoming Organizational Defenses* (Englewood Cliffs, NJ: Prentice-Hall, 1990).

CHAPTER 23

1. John P. Kotter, "Leading Change: Why Transformation Efforts Fail," *Harvard Business Review*, March–April 1995, p. 61.
2. Dave Ulrich, "A New Mandate for Human Resources," *Harvard Business Review*, January–February 1998, p. 131.

CHAPTER 25

1. Alex Korb, "The Grateful Brain," *Psychology Today*, November 20, 2012; http://www.psychologytoday.com/blog/prefrontal-nudity/201211/the-grateful-brain.

Index

About the Author

Roxi Bahar Hewertson is CEO of Highland Consulting Group, Inc., an entrepreneur, and a former adjunct faculty member at Cornell University's School of Industrial and Labor Relations.